The Alaska Geographic Society

THE ALASKA GEOGRAPHIC SOCIETY is a nonprofit organization exploring new frontiers of knowledge across the lands of the polar rim, learning how other men and other countries live in their Norths, putting the geography book back in the classroom, exploring new methods of teaching and learning—sharing in the excitement of discovery in man's wonderful new world north of 51°16'.

MEMBERS OF THE SOCIETY RECEIVE *Alaska Geographic*, a quality magazine in color which devotes each quarterly issue to monographic in-depth coverage of a northern geographic region or resource-oriented subject.

MEMBERSHIP DUES in The Alaska Geographic Society are $20 for initiation and the first year, $16 thereafter. (Eighty percent of the first year's dues is for a one-year subscription to *Alaska Geographic*.) Order from The Alaska Geographic Society, Box 4-EEE, Anchorage, Alaska 99509; (907) 243-1484.

MATERIAL SOUGHT: The editors of *Alaska Geographic* seek a wide variety of informative material on the lands north of 51°16' on geographic subjects—anything to do with resources and their uses (with heavy emphasis on quality color photography)—from Alaska, Northern Canada, Siberia, Japan—all geographic areas that have a relationship to Alaska in a physical or economic sense. We do not want material done in excessive scientific terminology. A query to the editors is suggested. Modest payments are made for all material upon publication.

CHANGE OF ADDRESS: The post office does not automatically forward *Alaska Geographic* when you move. To insure continuous service, notify us six weeks before moving. Send us your new address and zip code (and moving date), your old address and zip code, and if possible send a mailing label from a copy of *Alaska Geographic*. Send this information to Alaska Geographic Mailing Offices, 130 Second Avenue South, Edmonds, Washington 98020.

Second-class postage paid at Edmonds, Washington 98020.
Printed in U.S.A.

ALASKA GEOGRAPHIC

VOL. 4, NO. 3, 1977

KODIAK, Island of Change

COMPILED AND EDITED
by Nancy Freeman

WITH ASSISTANCE FROM
Gerry Atwell, Tom Casey, Donald W. Clark,
Roy Craft, Bill Donaldson, Dave Kennedy, Kodiak
Historical Society, Jack Lechner, Guy Powell,
Chris Reichert, Roger Smith, Frank Van Hulle,
Sam Welch.

Editors: Robert A. Henning, C. H. Rosenthal, Barbara Olds, Ed Reading
Designed by Roselyn Pape
CartoGraphics by Jon.Hersh

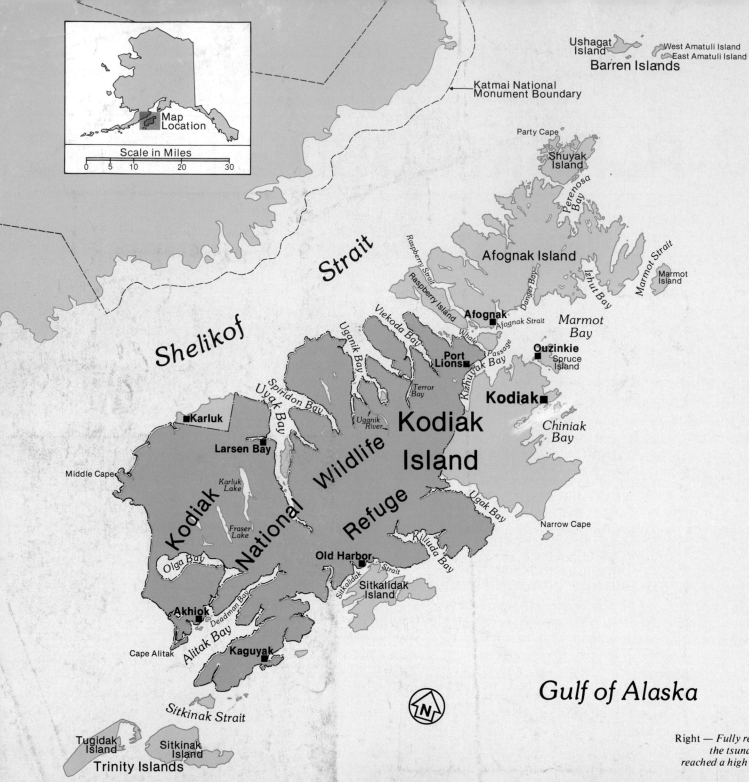

Ushagat
Island

West Amatuli Island

East Amatuli Island

Barren Islands

Katmai National
Monument Boundary

Party Cape

**Shuyak
Island**

*Perenosa
Bay*

Raspberry Strait

Raspberry Island

Afognak Island

Marmot
Strait

Marmot
Island

Strait

Danger Bay

Izhut Bay

Afognak

Afognak Strait

*Marmot
Bay*

Whale

Shelikof

Viekoda Bay

Uganik Bay

**Port
Lions**

Passage

Kizhuyak Bay

Ouzinkie

Spruce
Island

*Terror
Bay*

Kodiak

Spiridon Bay

Uyak Bay

*Uganik
River*

Kodiak

*Chiniak
Bay*

Karluk

Island

Larsen Bay

*Karluk
Lake*

Middle Cape

Kodiak

National

Wildlife

Refuge

*Fraser
Lake*

Ugak Bay

Narrow Cape

Olga Bay

Kiliuda Bay

Old Harbor

Strait

Sitkalidak

**Sitkalidak
Island**

Akhiok

Deadman Bay

Alitak Bay

Kaguyak

Cape Alitak

Gulf of Alaska

Sitkinak Strait

**Tugidak
Island**

**Sitkinak
Island**

Trinity Islands

Right — *Fully recovered from the disastrous 1964 earthquake,
the tsunamis and subsidence that followed, Kodiak has
reached a high point of economic stability. (Dick Sundbaum)*

Map
Location

Scale in Miles

0   5   10   20   30

KODIAK, Island of Change

4

Foreword

On a rain-whipped night, black as the bottom of a fisherman's boot, Kodiak can be bleak and forbidding. But when the sun warms its shores, however briefly, the spectacle is stunning: the bluest of oceans, loosely strung with emerald islands and guarded by great iron peaks, green or white, depending on the season.

Catapulted from one natural disaster to another, Kodiak Islanders have evolved as a feisty, independent and resilient people. They have long received wave after wave of adventurers, first seeking sea otters, then whales, later salmon and halibut and today, crab and shrimp. Tomorrow it will be bottomfish, perhaps, and certainly oil.

Each wave has brought change; some of it good. Whatever brings the newcomer, the beauty of this land and its people will hold him fast.

—*Nancy Freeman*

Whipped by a williwaw, tiny water droplets produce sea smoke above the ocean's surface. Unpredictable williwaws, sudden rushes of air spilling off Kodiak's coastal mountains, can carry winds in excess of 100 mph and represent a special hazard to commercial fishermen and sports sailors. (Gary Dobos)

1

The Distant Archipelago

Sixteen major islands form the Kodiak archipelago, stretching through 10,500 square miles on the western edge of the Gulf of Alaska. These rugged islands rise abruptly from the ocean floor and extend approximately 260 miles from the Barren Islands on the north to Chirikof Island on the south. Fifty miles south of the southern tip of the Kenai Peninsula and about 40 miles east of the Alaska Peninsula, the island group is aligned in a northeast-southwest direction, a trend formed by the Kodiak mountains. The mountains are a structural, southwestward continuation of the mountains of the Kenai Peninsula. Rocky peaks in the chain generally range from 2,000 to 3,500 feet and few reach more than

Sunrise at Karluk Lake, a historic salmon fishery, near the center of western Kodiak Island. (Gerry Atwell, U.S. Fish & Wildlife Service)

7

4,000 feet. On Kodiak Island the ridges and coastlines are ice-rounded and local relief generally varies from between 1,000 and 2,000 feet. Only the western part of Kodiak Island, characterized by many broad valleys and coastal lowlands, exhibits a relatively subdued relief. Most of the region's coastline is intricately outlined by deep, narrow, glacially scoured straits and fjords with numerous branching arms and scattered islets.

During glacial periods, this island group was a center of vigorous ice action, and from the higher mountains glaciers that almost completely covered the land pushed out to sea in all directions. The present topographical forms of the islands are largely the product of severe glacial erosion. (The fjords are so numerous that no area on Kodiak Island is more than 15 miles from tidewater.)

The Kodiak Island group has a total land area of nearly 5,000 square miles and is mostly uninhabited. Individual islands range in size from mere rocks to Kodiak Island—about 100 miles long and up to 60 miles wide—that covers more than 3,500 square miles. Afognak, the second-largest island, has an area of about 700 square miles. Other major islands are: Sitkalidak, 117 square miles; Sitkinak, 91; Raspberry, 82; Tugidak, 71; Shuyak, 69; Uganik, 57; Chirikof, 51; Marmot, 24; Spruce, 17; Whale, 14; Amook, 13; Ban, 11; and Ushagat and Aiaktalik, 7 square miles each.

More than half of the region's total area lies within federal land reserves: Kodiak National Wildlife Refuge on Kodiak Island (2,840 square miles); Chugach National Forest on Afognak Island (700 square miles); and the U.S. Coast Guard Reservation on Kodiak Island (53.2 square miles). In addition, about 480 square miles of land in the island group are covered by federal grazing leases.

Seaward of the Kodiak archipelago, the continental shelf averages 75 miles in width and covers a total area of more than 20,000 square miles.

Chilled by a quartering wind and helped along by an outgoing tide, a fishing boat moves into Chiniak Bay from the shelter of Kodiak's harbor. (Gary Dobos)

2

The Beginning

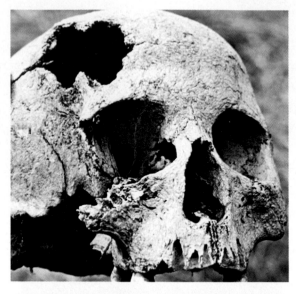

An island was born out of the sea when ancient rock layers were buckled and thrust upward at the edge of the continent eons ago. It was shaped for many ages by the pounding waves and lashing North Pacific gales. Then, tens of thousands of years ago, the rains turned to more snow than could melt each year, and the snow to ice that flowed out of the highlands to the sea. Kodiak finally emerged from the ice age carved by glaciers to the intricate rocky shape we know today.

Kodiak's history has been linked with the sea and man's use of the island as a base to exploit the sea's resources. First there were Native hunters and fishers, then came Russians seeking sea mammal pelts, and finally American salters, packers and freezers of fish.

We do not know who the first people of Kodiak were; they left behind nothing except distinctive stone tools and weapon tips. By the time of European discovery in the 18th century, new-

Clockwise from upper left — A Koniag skull washed out of a bank at Kiavak Bay. The puncture indicates that this early Kodiak inhabitant died violently. (Gerry Atwell, USF&WS) Reproductions of incised slate figurine tablets common to an early culture on Kodiak. (D.W. Clark) Remains of a Russian flintlock found at Kiavak Bay. (Gerry Atwell, USF&WS) Chipped projectile points found on Kodiak and identified as being from the Ocean Bay I and transition periods. (D.W. Clark)

Right — An early spring beach scene. The dead, brown grass will become lush and green as the season progresses. (Gary Dobos)

comers, the Koniags—a skin-boat people, members of a widely distributed Eskimo family—possessed the island.

But the resources of the sea, especially the sea otter and fur seal, attracted the Russians. They became masters of the island but for a while the Native culture endured, exerting its pre-eminence in maritime lifeways. The Russians found that the Koniags, often using their own techniques, were adept at catching the prized sea otter and at preparing large enough quantities of salmon to feed the colony. But the Russians introduced a new religion, and centralized political and commercial systems.

Natives and colonial Russians alike had to adjust to a new administration after 1867. But in the villages the transition was gradual and the occasional newcomer from the United States mixed with the old families. Russian and Creole lifeways, for which the Orthodox church was central, persisted and commercial hunting of marine fur bearers and subsistence fishing continued. American commercial interests that came to Kodiak and the islands also explored other marine resources: whales, codfish, and salmon salting, a prelude to the canned salmon industry that flourished from the 1880's onward.

After concentrating on producing canned salmon and relatively small volumes of herring for 75 years, new seafood markets were developed with the aid of a specialized technology that permitted the harvest of king crab, halibut, shrimp and tanner crab.

Kodiak has experienced brief or

11

A miniature, but functional stone lamp, adz blade and shaft abrader from the transition and Ocean Bay II periods on Kodiak, about 2500 B.C. (D.W. Clark)

minor roles as a beef and forest products producer and service center but it remains primarily a land of fishers and sea hunters who harvest many of the same resources that stimulated Europeans to seek the wealth of the island.

EARLY PREHISTORY

By at least 6,300 years ago maritime hunters and fishers were living on Kodiak and Afognak Islands. These people left the chipped flint points and knives of the Ocean Bay I culture—named for a locality on Sitkalidak Island, one of the Kodiak group. Predecessors of the Ocean Bay people may someday be discovered on Kodiak inasmuch as other parts of southwestern Alaska were occupied as early as 8,000 or 9,000 years ago. Eventually, any projection into the past will come to the time when the late ice age glaciers that covered Kodiak melted, freeing the islands for occupation, and, too, people in the North Pacific area had to develop, in some "halfway" situation, the specialized maritime economy required to safely reach and live in stormy island habitats. Envision a young hunter, perhaps 8,000 years ago, alone and afraid, paddling across Shelikof Strait to a land where there was neither friend nor foe—no one at all. But soon he, or others like him, returned to Kodiak with their families, to stay.

During the summer, Ocean Bay people camped at the mouths of streams in order to exploit the salmon runs, probably through the use of spears and traps. At the same time they continued

their principal pursuit which was the sea mammal chase. In addition to seals and sea lions, they took sea otter, porpoise, probably whales, fowl, and the occasional land mammal. Shellfish were gathered when available or when required. Presumably cod, sculpin and halibut were caught a short distance offshore, and bird rookeries were raided for eggs. This North Pacific maritime type of economy has, with variations, forever been that of Kodiak.

Close relatives of these early islanders lived on the adjacent mainland, but we do not know with certainty whether the Ocean Bay people were Eskimos, Aleuts or even Indians.

At first, Ocean Bay I people rarely ground slate, but eventually, about 2700 B.C., they took a greater interest in the production of slate implements—forever after to be a distinguishing characteristic of the region—particularly bayonet-shaped points and lances, and large stemmed knives. Within a couple centuries some groups on Kodiak had almost completely given up chert (flint) flaking, thus giving rise to the Ocean Bay II culture. On the mainland opposite and also among some island communities, however, the new slate technology simply was added to the flaked implements which continued to be made.

During the second millennium B.C. a new culture developed in outer Cook Inlet and on Kodiak. This was the Kachemak tradition, which through two and a half millennia became progressively more elaborate and then was transformed into Pacific Eskimo. (Here a tradition is the lifeway of a particular people viewed over a long period taking into account changes through time.) Continuity from Ocean Bay to the Kachemak tradition, so named from the bay in Cook Inlet where it was defined early in the 1930's, is open to varied interpretations. We are not certain whether it developed from the Ocean Bay tradition or whether it represents a different people who invaded Kodiak; nor are we certain that the Kachemak people were Eskimos, although that most likely is the case.

The earliest Kachemak people had an unelaborated implement kit. They flaked and ground stone, although usually without duplicating the Ocean Bay II styles and techniques. Characteristic among their simple implements is a stone cobble weight grooved plummet-style about one end. Through time, essentially the first millennium B.C., material culture became more complex but still there was little elaboration of implements and artwork. Middle and late Kachemak people were active fishermen and to this end they produced tremendous numbers of notched pebbles for net sinkers and several varieties of larger notched and grooved stones mainly to be used on lines at sea. Kachemak culture continued to develop and reached its zenith during the first millennium A.D.

The distinctiveness of late Kachemak culture is seen best when it is contrasted with the succeeding Koniag culture. Although there is considerable similarity in the types of implements used, late Kachemak produced better-finished tools and hunting equipment. Furthermore, many styles changed, generally to simpler ones in the Koniag phase. Late Kachemak people adorned themselves with a large variety of beads, pendants, figurines, labrets, and ornamental pins produced in bone, ivory, jet, shell, a soft red stone, and marble. Their most noteworthy productions were massive pecked stone lamps with human figures, animals, and female breasts carved in the bowl in high relief or on the exterior in lower relief. Occupation sites and refuse deposits are replete with cut and drilled human bones, trophy heads, dismembered burials, artificial eyes, and other evidence for varied practices with the dead and, also, probable cannibalism.

At this time the adjacent side of the Alaska Peninsula was occupied by a somewhat different people, although contact across Shelikof Strait continued and the two peoples probably intermarried, traded for island and mainland products, and had generally similar lifeways.

EVENTS LEADING TO THE HISTORIC KONIAG ESKIMO

To reconstruct the formation or origins of the historic Koniags of Kodiak it is necessary to speculate a series of events.

Kodiak appears to have had active lines of communication to the southern Bering Sea region and also northeast to Cook Inlet and Prince William Sound. Communication would have consisted of trading partnerships, exchange festivals and visiting, intermarriage, and raids. Seemingly, soon after 1000 A.D. people from outer Cook Inlet and areas farther east were moving in on friendly villages, family by family, first to Afognak and then to Kodiak Island proper. It is difficult to say who assimilated whom, but the unelaborated material culture of the newcomers, and new kinds of activities which they brought, prevailed. The vapor sweat bath, among new activities, became very popular, wood was split with a new type of heavy grooved stone splitting adz, and during one of their rituals people now made and discarded numerous incised slate pebble figurines. Hunters pecked figures of whales, faces, and other designs—called petroglyphs—into rock exposures.

Similarly, on southwestern Kodiak people were coming from the Alaska Peninsula and the southern Bering Sea coast in such numbers that they were able to introduce new practices like pottery making. The hybrid development of prehistoric Koniag culture, illustrated by the fact that pottery never was adopted on the northeastern half of Kodiak, continued to be apparent up to the time of European contact and probably was maintained through differing contacts with people located, respectively, to the west and northeast of Kodiak.

Thus, about 1100 A.D. the Kachemak tradition was succeeded by the Koniag culture which had developed through a combination of population movement, amalgamation, and rapid change in habits and stylistic preferences. As seen from the Pacific, a feature of this period is the reaffirmation of cultural bonds with Bering Sea Eskimos, but these form only one component of Koniag culture. Aconite poison whaling, mummies secreted in caves, and petroglyph art are part of another, ancient North Pacific, perspective.

Actual archaeological procedure has been the reverse of the narrative outlined here and starts from the analysis of the top levels of two abandoned Koniag village sites visited by Captain Lisianski in 1805, and then progresses backwards through time to older levels in these and other, more ancient, sites.

KONIAGS AND RUSSIANS MEET

When the Russian *promyshleniki* reached the southern mainland coast of Alaska they found a series of Eskimo groups now collectively called the Pacific Eskimo, the most populous of which were the Koniags who possessed Kodiak Island and part of the adjacent Alaska Peninsula. Some explorers appear to have known the Koniags by that name from contact with their Aleutian neighbors even before they had sailed to Kodiak. Others say that the inhabitants of Kodiak called themselves Kikhtahgmitt or "island people." The Koniags

and their mortal enemies the Aleuts spoke different languages, but due to common historical and cultural processes during the Russian period, and to similarities in physical appearance and lifeways, the term Aleut has been extended to many south Alaskan Eskimo groups.

The Koniags vigorously resisted Glotov in 1763 when he spent the winter on the south end of Kodiak; later, in 1776, Bragin was similarly dealt with and was forced to leave the island. Shelikov finally forcibly overcame Koniag resistance, established a post at Three Saints Bay on Kodiak in 1784, took hostages, and subjugated the population. The Natives were organized into a work force under appointed chiefs and Russian overseers. All men and women were required to work for the Russian company for a certain period of years. This included service in a sea otter

hunting brigade or at fox trapping and work in small settlements to secure a diverse array of natural provisions for the Russian communities. Men and hunting parties were freely dispersed over coastal Alaska and California. These demands and dispersals severely disrupted the Native lifeway and are among the factors responsible for a rapid population decline. From an estimated population of 8,000 at the time of first sustained contact in 1784 the Koniags decreased to about 2,500 persons by the middle of the 19th century where they stood, more or less, for the next century.

A number of explorers have written accounts of early Koniag lifeways, but neither these accounts nor the present space allow us to put together the complete story of Koniag culture. Perhaps, however, a partial description will convey an impression of former times.

A 1916 photo of the "Passage at Kodiak," where Baranov's hunters once paddled out to sea a thousand strong. (C.L. Andrews Collection, University of Alaska Archives)

EARLY TRADITIONAL KONIAG LIFEWAYS

All is quiet, then a mobile gray mass emerges from the depths breaking the water—a sharp jab: the wounded whale dives, the rear paddler in the two-hatch *bidarka* backs off to avoid danger, and the hunters are gone too, back to the shore to wait quietly several days for the dead whale to float. We no longer know whether the efficacy of the dart, a slate-tipped feathered shaft 5 feet long, was due to the aconite poison smeared on it during secret rites or due to inflamation produced by salt water and the 12-inch-long ground slate tip. Unlike harpoon whaling, no physical tie was maintained with the whale, but the deeply embayed coast of Kodiak was preeminently suited for recovering drift whales.

Another drama takes place when a party of hunters in their kayaks (*bidarkas*) surrounds a sea otter: "the prey [is] so sure, that scarcely one animal out of a hundred can save itself from its pursuers" writes Lisianski. In addition to the cooperative surround method of hunting with harpoon-arrows and darts, sea otter also were clubbed when they were forced ashore during storms.

Seal hunting was of considerable importance for food, oil, and hides as also were, variously, the salmon fishery, salt-water fishery, and whaling. Harbor seals were harpooned from kayaks or from the shore after being attracted within range through a decoy consisting of a seal head-shaped helmet

or inflated sealskin, were clubbed at hauling grounds, or were trapped and entangled with large nets. Two other important marine sources of food and raw material—porpoises and sea lions—were harpooned. Sea birds were taken with a variety of projectiles and in nets, but the bola was not used.

Land mammals were of considerably lesser importance, although the Kodiak bear, foxes and otter were trapped or hunted, and caribou were sought on occasional trips to the Alaska Peninsula. Where locally available, ground squirrels were intensively snared for pelts to make parkas.

Too little is known about fisheries considering the major place they had in Koniag subsistence. Denizens of the sea, particularly cod, halibut, and sculpin were hooked. Salmon fishing was concentrated at spawning streams where, at weirs located near summer settlements, several species were speared, gaffed, or harpooned and dried.

Economic activities followed a natural annual cycle which probably formed a calendar for other aspects of Koniag life, although no detailed account of the annual cycle is recorded. In the autumn, after the salmon season and sea mammal hunting, families returned to their main settlements to prepare for the winter festivities.

The main or winter villages were located behind headlands, in the lee of small islands, or in small embayments close to the outer coasts of the islands. Dwellings were not numerous, but several families, up to 20 persons, lived in each house, and a settlement easily could hold 100 to 200 persons. Early on a good morning one could find the male residents contemplatively sitting upon the turf and straw-covered roof of their home gazing at the sunrise. Inside, the main or common room, with its central hearth and unkept floor, served as the kitchen while families slept and found privacy in appended, better-kept, floored side chambers. The common room also could be used as a workshop and for ceremonies in villages that did not have a hall. The private side rooms were heated with hot rocks and one was employed for vapor sweat baths which were taken by both sexes.

The composition of a household has not been recorded, but we may expect to find there several sisters and their husbands and families, their parents—the dominant couple although now past

Petroglyph from Afognak Island. Other examples of the area's many rock drawings are at far left, facing page and at the bottom of page 16. (D. W. Clark)

middle age—any unmarried brothers and sisters, and an assortment of peripheral persons, among them poor relatives and foster children whose status was little better than that of the occasional slave which had been purchased or taken in a raid, and also visiting friends or partners and possibly aged grandparents.

Departure from the household often was by death which, however, did not completely terminate relationships with the living as the dead were kept at hand in a sealed side chamber of the house or were interred within the settlement area. Rich persons or those in special categories might be taken to secluded places and preserved, sometimes for participation in secret whaling rituals. The deceased later would be honored with a memorial feast at the next winter celebrations.

A considerable battery of ceremonies, dances, masked performances and feasts followed in rapid succession in the early winter as long as the food reserves permitted. Among these were the memorial feast for the dead, an animal increase ceremony, and invitational potlatches to which other villages were invited to trade and socialize. These, other public gatherings, and restricted ceremonies were held in the men's hall or *kashim* which was built by a rich leader (*anayugak* or "chief").

Although a position of leadership was one of high status, and might be inherited, it had to be maintained on a personal basis. The deference shown to chiefs probably was due more to their influence and economic power than to any formalized office or rank. In personal undertakings, but not in communal proceedings decided in a gathering, a man followed his own will.

Other special roles or occupations were those of the shaman or medicine man, the "wise-man," the curer, and, too, possibly the whaler. Shamans would forecast the success or proper timing of an undertaking, forecast or control the weather, undertake curing, and could, for instance, ascertain the well-being of a far-away relative. Contact with the supernatural was attained through trances, but masks and dolls also were employed. There was no special costume, but a garment might be reversed and so might sex in the case of the male transvestite medicine man. Women also could be shamans. Much curing was done, however, not by shamans but by healers, usually women, whose range of bloodletting practices approached acupuncture. They also knew several herbal cures and employed "extraction" methods to suck out the cause of illness. Others, the wise men or *kaseks* who have been terminologically equated to Russian priests, organized and conducted the religious ceremonies and saw to the perpetuation of the requisite knowledge.

—Donald W. Clark

About the Author

Born in Portland, Oregon, Donald W. Clark moved to Kodiak at age 9 in 1941. Clark has degrees in geology (University of Alaska, Fairbanks) and anthropology (University of Wisconsin, Madison), specializing in archaeology. He presently lives in Ottawa, Ontario, and works for the Archaeological Survey of Canada, a division of the National Museum of Man. Clark's interests are primarily in archaeology and culture history. He has done field work in the District of Mackenzie and in the Kodiak Island and Koyukuk River regions of Alaska. These regions are the subject of the monographs and many articles Clark has published in professional journals.

The Russian Period and After

The fifty-two men who signed on to sail with Baranov to Russia's new colony on Kodiak Island in 1790 had to swear before the Okhotsk commander that they (1) were in their right minds; (2) had no venereal diseases; (3) would remain faithful to the Russian Imperial government; and (4) would stay with the company for 5 years.

Through Baranov's energy, Kodiak was transformed from a wilderness outpost into an oasis of civilized life. The fur trade flourished and Kodiak continued as a major commercial center even after the Russian capital was moved to Sitka in 1794.

With the formation of the Russian-American Company in 1799, Russian control of Alaska was consolidated and Kodiak prospered.

"The village of Saint Paul, or Kadiak, contained in 1880 about 400 inhabitants, a large proportion of whom were Creoles. Here were built the stores and warehouses of the Alaska Commercial Company, the Western Fur and Trading Company, and the barracks formerly occupied by United States troops. . . . The people are probably better circumstanced than those of their own status in other portions of America. Labor is abundant and fairly paid; food is cheap and abundant; there are no paupers in their midst; no lawyers or tax collectors; and all are at liberty to make use of unoccupied land.

"At Wood[y] Island, opposite to Saint Paul, is a thriving settlement, the inhabitants of which support themselves in the summer by hunting and in winter by cutting and storing ice. In order to develop the latter industry was built the first road constructed in Alaska, comprising the circuit of the island, a distance of about 13 miles.

"The village of Three Saints, where it will be remembered Shelikov landed from a vessel of that name in 1784, and founded the pioneer colony in Russian America, now contains about 300 inhabitants. They were in Shelikov's days the finest sea otter grounds and are now perhaps the finest halibut grounds in Alaska.

"The village of Afognak, on the island of the same name, separated by a narrow channel from the northern shore of Kadiak, is one of the most thriving settlements in Alaska. Though mountainous, and in some parts thickly wooded, the cutting of timber and firewood being one of the chief industries, it contains many spots suitable for pasture and agriculture. Boatbuilding is also a profitable occupation. Many of the inhabitants, who now muster about 350, live in substantial frame houses, this being one of the few places in the territory where any considerable number of dwellings other than log huts are to be found."

(Bancroft, *History of Alaska,* 1730-1885)

Above — *Alexander Baranov, appointed by the Russian-American Company to head its operations in Alaska, served with energy and distinction from 1790 to 1818. He moved the Russian capital from Kodiak to Sitka in 1794. (Reprinted from* The ALASKA JOURNAL®*)*
Below — *Paul's Harbor (Saint Paul Harbor) and an 1842 view of Kodiak, then one of Alaska's major settlements. (Reprinted from* The ALASKA JOURNAL®*)*

From major operations bases at Kodiak and Sitka, Russian developers concentrated on fur gathering but also attempted to develop some of Alaska's mineral resources, such as this coal mine on the Kenai Peninsula. (The Yale University Library, reprinted from The ALASKA JOURNAL®)

Tanneries were established at Karluk and Uyak Bay. Brickyards were operating at Kodiak and Long Island by the early 1880's. Salteries were established at Karluk River, the world's greatest salmon producer.

By 1835 the rich whaling grounds around Kodiak Island were discovered and, until 1869, most of the whale oil produced by the American whaling fleet was secured from these waters. Whaling peaked in the far North Pacific between 1846 and 1851 but the industry continued until the 20th century. Kodiak benefitted for a time when the use of whale oil as a base for margarine caused a brief resurgence of the industry in 1910. By 1914 the great whaling fleets were nearly gone and the industry was largely confined to shore stations that produced fertilizer.

By the late 1850's, the Russian-American Company was in trouble. "Company affairs," wrote Russian naval officer K. I. Nedel'kovich, "are not in a brilliant position at the present time; there is a depression in the chief wares, furs and tea, which—it is said—is carried in enormous quantities to St. Petersburg by different routes. Therefore the company is now trying to observe the greatest economy in everything."

"The Chief manager has even received word not to raise any of the employees' wages before the end of their term of service, to try to deduct the debts from indebted employees sooner, and in as far as possible to order fewer goods from Victoria and California, which because of the war in America have risen to a great degree. . . . Here [in the colonies] private inhabitants all suffer from the destruction of property and settlements, and there is a depression in all internal products. . . . And now moreover they have intentionally ceased to send many things from Russia, so at the present there is not even rye flour—something, in my opin-

Okhotsk, the major port in eastern Siberia, was the principal embarkation point for Alaska-bound men and materials during the Russian period. (Reprinted from The ALASKA JOURNAL®)

ion, highly necessary for the Russians, especially for the working men." (Fedorova, *The Russian Population in Alaska and California*, 1973.)

Depletion of the sea otter diminished Alaska's value and was one reason for its eventual sale to the United States. Not everyone cheered. An editorial in *Harper's Magazine* in 1867 chided, "There may be immense advantages in the acquisition of this Russian desert; but they are not suspected by the country, and they are thus far carefully concealed by the government."

Eighty years of Russian dominion left a deep mark. By Russian accounts, there were more than 8,000 Koniags of both sexes on Kodiak Island on May 25, 1799. Originally distributed in 65 villages throughout the island, the Koniags reportedly were regrouped into only 7 villages. Food resources were low and the population continued to diminish. When the United States acquired Alaska in 1867, the Koniags had vanished as a distinct ethnographic group. By 1929, according to U.S. census, the Kodiak recording district had a population of 1,729.

"After the transfer of Alaska to the United States," writes Yule Chaffin (*Koniag to King Crab*, 1967), "the men began to hunt sea otter with rifles instead of spears. The steam launches and schooners of the white traders carried the hunters and their *bidarkas* to the hunting grounds. The sea otter herds were depleted rapidly in this manner in the 1880's. . . . Few otter were to be found in 1911 when hunting them was prohibited and a $500 fine imposed on anyone caught in possession of a sea otter skin."

And the depression which began in 1895 was to severely affect Kodiak's position as a major shipping center. The economy bottomed out in 1897 and several shipping companies went bankrupt. But in July 1897, the steamer *Portland* arrived in Seattle with 68 miners carrying $960,000 in gold. A mad rush for the Klondike and Alaska began.

With the emergence of Nome as a major gold mining center, Kodiak Island became one of the main stopping points on the way north. When the gold fever subsided in 1903, shipping in Kodiak slowed with it but the island's economy continued to grow until the Novarupta (Mount Katmai) eruption in 1912 impacted salmon streams, choked them with ash, and disrupted the island's major industry.

Recovery was relatively slow but by 1920 the salmon and halibut industries were again on top. Then after World War II began, defense installations were established throughout the island; and the population of Greater Kodiak increased from 2,000 in 1939 to more than 6,000 in 1950.

Though the war had brought most Alaskan fisheries exploration to a standstill, over at Port Wakefield on Raspberry Island, northeast of Kodiak, the Lowell Wakefield family was beginning to experiment with king crab. At the other end of the island, the Suryan family was also putting up a few hundred cases of king crab. By 1955, Wakefield produced 85% of the U.S. catch of king crab. These pioneers and others led the way for the newest and one of the most hazardous of the world's major fisheries. Alaska has also become the great western producer of shrimp—with landings rising steadily since the fifties—and most of it is delivered at Kodiak.

Despite the destruction in 1964 when tsunamis flooded the island in the wake of the largest major earthquake to hit North America, Kodiak was able to practically rebuild within 5 years.

The city of Kodiak has remained almost precisely upon the site of the Russian settlement that Baranov established in 1794. Today, the modern community has a population of about 9,300 boroughwide and continues as a top U.S. fishing port. Here Alaska's largest fleets bring in huge landings of salmon, halibut, shrimp and crab; and local fishermen are experimenting with specialty packs, trying their own hand at processing and marketing and gearing up for bottomfish.

While living marine resources still form the largest segment of the economy, the island also has agriculture development and an increasing interest in the forest products industry. The Coast Guard Support Center—already the largest in Alaska—is expanding; and what is frankly considered to be the coming boom—oil production—is rushing in on the next wave.

—*Nancy Freeman*

A double-headed eagle, crest of the Russian empire, was buried in carefully marked locations by Russian explorers to authenticate Russian claims to new territory. This example, some parts are missing, is in the Alaska State Museum. (University of Alaska, reprinted from The ALASKA JOURNAL®*)*

During the first week in June [1912] Katmai Volcano, in southwestern Alaska, which had generally been believed to be an extinct volcano, unexpectedly burst into violent eruption and continued active for three days. . . . So dense was the cloud cast into the heavens that the people in the village of Kadiak, 100 miles distant, were in total darkness for two days. All the crops on Kadiak Island were destroyed by the ashes; the fish in the sea and in the rivers were killed and all water supplies were poisoned. . . .

—**National Geographic**

▼BEFORE

4

Eyewitness to Disaster

After centuries of quiet, Novarupta volcano—near Katmai village—unleashed a fury described as the most violent in recorded history. Coarse, gray ash reached Uyak, 58 miles from the mountain, at 3:30 p.m. June 6, 1912, and at Kodiak at 5 p.m. Soon afterward darkness settled down over an area of several thousand square miles.

Writing of the experience later, Hildred Erskine said, "The ash was falling so heavily that our greatest anxiety was whether we should be able to get another breath. The gases were nauseating and to add to our terror,

Left — Walter Metrokin and fellow trapper "Big" Andrew Yakashoff, far left, were packers on an early expedition to Katmai. A post-eruption flood sheared off many trees at ash level. Right — Before and after photographs of Kodiak and a waterfront detail showing the effects of the Katmai eruption. (All photos, Eli Metrokin)

Kodiak, Alaska.
(Before the eruption of "Katmai" Volcano)

Kodiak, Alaska.
(Before the eruption of "Katmai" V...

↓AFTER↑

Kodiak, Alaska.
(After the eruption of "Katmai"...

earthquake shock became almost continuous. The terrible bombardment grew louder and louder; and the ash sifted through cracks around the windows and doors. . . . We were sure our time had come. There was a slight lull at ten that night and we thought maybe the worst was over. Our relief was short-lived and for four long hours the noise, gas and shocks became almost unbearable.''

It was the village doctor who came to fetch Hildred and her cousin (both schoolteachers) early the next morning to board the revenue cutter *Manning,* tied up at the Kodiak dock. ''We tied dampened cheese-cloth over our faces, but the ash penetrated several thicknesses of the material. We followed fences and ditches and somehow reached our destination. The officers of the *Manning* turned on the search light, but the ash was so dense that even its powerful light gave no aid. . . .''

Things grew worse by 4 a.m. Saturday so the ship's whistle sounded blast upon blast to warn the villagers to come aboard: ''Not all were able to board one ship, so most of the men were put aboard the barge *St. James,* which was towed by the tug *Printer.* We had 500 men, women and children on the *Manning.* Nearly all suffered from nervous shock and were in fear of their lives.'' The *Manning* departed about 10 a.m. Saturday and anchored off Woody Island, about 2 miles from Kodiak.

Hildred wrote, ''the men who had shoveled ash from the decks were worn out and their eyes were in a pitiful condition; the ash had penetrated the bandages they wore over their eyes and had painfully cut their eyeballs. A little native woman, ill with tuberculosis . . . somehow found her way to the ship, but died very shortly. . . .''

On Monday the *Manning* returned to Kodiak and villagers discovered ash 18 inches deep on level ground but many, many feet deep from slides off the cliffs.

''One house at the base of a hill,'' Hildred wrote, ''was completely wrecked by the ash. Many roofs collapsed from the great weight and the water mains were so choked that new mains had to be laid.'' The crew of the *Manning* distilled water for drinking and cooking.

''Lakes that had had a depth of five feet were completely filled and have never since been lakes. Ptarmigan were killed in their nesting season; trout were completely destroyed in the lakes; low bush berries which had been so plentiful were destroyed. Several of the famous

Below — *Professor Robert Griggs and an assistant prepare to photograph Katmai's caldera.* Bottom — *Volcanic ash piled against a Kodiak residence. (Both photos, Eli Metrokin)*

The U.S.R.C. McCulloch *was one of a fleet of relief vessels that brought aid to terror-stricken Kodiak residents after the Katmai eruption. (Eli Metrokin)*

U.S.R.C. "McCulloch", Relief Ship at Kodiak, Alaska. (During the eruption of "Katmai" Volcano, June 6 to 8, 1912

Kodiak bears came down to the beaches seeking food.

"One of the most disastrous results was the fact that when the ash filled the streams, it made it impossible to tell where the streams had been and the dampened ash became quicksand. One man sank in the sand to his armpits before rescuers found him. It took only half an hour for him to sink so deep, but it took two and a half hours to dig him out. His body was blue from the pressure and he later died from the effects of the ordeal.

"For weeks we dug ashes out of our houses, but every time the wind blew from the west, the dust was so thick and the gases so bad we were about ready to give up. . . . All that summer we had occasional earthquakes but none that caused any real damage. . . ."

Professor Robert F. Griggs, who was to lead several expeditions to Mount Katmai and its environs for the National Geographic Society, said he could not believe his eyes when he returned to Kodiak 2 years after the eruption. "Where before had been barren ash was now rich grass as high as one's head. Everyone agrees that the eruption was the best thing that ever happened to Kodiak. In the words of our hotel keeper, never was any such grass known before, so high or early. No one ever believed the country could grow so many berries, nor so large, before the ash."

—*Nancy Freeman*

Right — *Captain R.C. Parker, General C.H. Corlett and Captain J. Perry, left to right, were commanders of the Navy's Alaska sector, Fort Greely, Kodiak, and Kodiak Naval Air Base, respectively, at the beginning of World War II.* Below — *Soldiers in formation offer a salute to General Corlett in front of the Fort Greely barracks. Soldiers spent their first winter on the island in pyramidal tents but wooden barracks were available for the second winter. (Both photos, Roy Craft)*

5

Kodiak—
The War Years

When a military-naval-air base, with more than 10,000 soldiers, sailors, airmen, construction workers and even a sprinkling of Marines, was suddenly established at Kodiak in the months preceding World War II, it might have been supposed the little village would be overwhelmed.

It wasn't. The rugged individuals who had cast their lots on the island with the sturdy Aleuts and the descendants of early Russian colonists, took it in stride. Kodiak had weathered the Katmai eruption of 1912 when a shower of ash inundated the island, as it was in later years to weather an earthquake and seismic wave. It weathered the defense inundation with the same aplomb.

The town of Kodiak had a population of some 800 souls when the Navy began construction of a base in 1939, after defense officials belatedly recognized

Extra edition of the Kodiak Mirror *announcing the war's beginning. (Roy Craft)*

its potential as a strategic naval outpost. When the Army began moving in a year later with thousands of men, the little town was soon bursting at the seams. Nothing so explosive had happened since Catherine the Great of Russia sent Baranov to found a colony as a sea otter and sealing center. Prior to the defense buildup, Kodiak's economy was based principally on fish canneries and fisheries, although it was also a popular port of call for hunters seeking the great Kodiak bear.

In November, 1941, the month preceding Pearl Harbor, the town's population had boomed to an estimated 3,500. Transient construction laborers had filled the town to capacity and housing was far behind demand. The one hotel was full and had a long waiting list. The prime Navy contractor, Siems-Drake Puget Sound, housed many of its men in a series of contractors barracks and shacks in an area called Buskinville, and the Navy had pressed into service a retired cruise ship, the S.S. *Yale*, which housed workmen and supplied steam for the base. Some of the early arrivals were lucky enough to have found housing and had their families with them. Others, prior to Pearl Harbor, were making plans to bring their families north.

Business enterprises in the community were inadequate. Two general stores, which had been established for years, carried lines of groceries, hardware and dry goods. There were several variety stores, one drugstore, two photo shops, and an electrical appliance store, one fair restaurant and three or four short-order places. There was the Bank of Kodiak, a tiny bakery, a dry-cleaning and laundering establishment, two ice-cream fountains, a grocery, a meat market, several pool halls and numerous liquor stores and bars, most of them newly established.

The Mecca was the lone "nightclub," located in the rear of a saloon and its decor featured pseudo-Persian murals. It boasted a jukebox. Men unattended by ladies were not admitted. The main doors were kept locked and men fortunate enough to be accompanied by ladies—a scarcity—were admitted through a gate at the back of the bar.

There was also a "Chicken Inn" some distance from town, plus two theaters of wood-frame construction, a hospital, the Russian Orthodox church and a Community Baptist church. A weekly newspaper, the *Kodiak Mirror*, had been published for about 6 months. Type for the little tabloid was handset but a linotype machine had been ordered. Water systems were private enterprises. Most householders piped water from streams on the hillside. The sewer system was primitive. There was an elementary school and high school classes were held.

Busses ran between Kodiak and the burgeoning naval-military base and there were 126 licensed taxis, all of which ran back and forth to the base at $3 a trip each way or 50 cents per person when the cab was loaded. They did a big business with the soldiers and sailors on paydays and a big business all the time with the civilian laborers who enjoyed a higher pay scale.

The town of Kodiak had no telephone system but the Army and the contractors were running a line to the bank, the U.S. marshal's office and a few other key places. The U.S. Signal Office operated communications to and from the States and messages sent through the system were routed for delivery by Western Union or Postal Telegraph. Day rate was 22 cents a word with a 10-word limit. For night letters the rate was 20 cents a word and longer messages were accepted.

The defense buildup had changed Kodiak from a village that slept between salmon seasons to a boom town. But World War II was to change it even more dramatically.

It has been said that "war discovered Alaska." It can also be said that the war discovered Kodiak and brought it indelibly to the attention of Americans on the mainland. Millions suddenly became aware of Kodiak and its strategic value as the hilt of the 1,000-mile-long sword, the Aleutians, thrust at the mainland of Asia.

Pearl Harbor Day, December 7, 1941, was a day of high drama.

The naval air station and the military base, Fort Greely, had been on alert status for 2 weeks and all outposts and stations were manned, despite a limited supply of ammunition. (Military men who served at Fort Greely are still puzzled that at the time of the Japanese attack armed forces in Hawaii and the Philippines were caught flat-footed.)

At 10:10 a.m. Kodiak time, a message was received through Navy channels that the Japanese were attacking Pearl Harbor. Within minutes, a meeting was arranged between Brigadier General Charles H. Corlett, commander of the Fort Greely Army base, and Captain J. Perry, naval air station commander.

There was no overall command, so the two officers issued an order, signed by both, placing the base on a war footing and ordering a curfew and blackout of downtown Kodiak.

An aide was dispatched to carry the news to the town and the most likely spots for immediate announcements were the two movie houses, which ran almost around the clock. At each theater, the film was stopped and the officer stepped on stage and delivered the news that the Japanese had attacked Pearl Harbor, that naval and military personnel were to return immediately to their bases and that the town was to be darkened at night. Their authority over the civilian population was questionable but this was no time for legal niceties.

Their response to the announcements was typical of Kodiak. The audience cheered! The long wait was over. Far from panicking, military men and civilians shook hands, and many civilians made immediate vows to grow beards until the Japanese had been defeated. With the cooperation of U.S. Marshal Paul Herring, a 300-pounder who resembled one-time heavyweight champion Jess Willard, a curfew was initiated. The marshal was the law in Kodiak prior to statehood.

At the office of the little *Kodiak Mirror*, an extra was rushed out in about five hours to herald the outbreak of war. It was really a "flier" on 8½ x 11 paper but the type was handset and it hit the streets with distribution help from taxi drivers and Boy Scouts. The paper's press run was cut short when the old platen press jammed; the *Mirror* extra is now a valued collector's item.

While Kodiak was prepared to defend itself against a possible Japanese attack, the top commanders knew Alaska's military strength was inadequate. General Simon Bolivar Buckner was head of the Alaska Defense Command, with headquarters in Anchorage. He had pleaded, with little success, for air units, which he regarded as the key to island defense, and he had few planes at the time of Pearl Harbor.

Similarly, while naval bases were being established, few ships or air units were available to the Navy command. Had Kodiak been attacked during the early stages of the war, only a handful of planes could have been sent up to meet the Japanese.

For practical purposes, World War II in Alaska and the Aleutians embraced the period December 7, 1941, the day war was declared, to August 15, 1943, when American and Canadian forces occupied Kiska without opposition, a fact that made it obvious the Japanese had abandoned hopes of using the Aleutian Islands as a springboard to the U.S. mainland.

A simple chronology of the Aleutian campaign includes: the Japanese attack on Dutch Harbor June 3, 1942; American occupation of Adak and the estab-

Above — *The late Joe E. Brown, famed comedian, was one of the first entertainers to visit military and naval personnel on Kodiak.* Upper right — *Principals in the development of Kodiak's military preparedness, left to right, General Butler, Army Air Corps, Admiral Kinkaid, General Corlett, commander of Fort Greely and General Simon Bolivar Buckner, head of the Alaska Defense Command.* Right — *An 8-foot Kodiak bear that was shot after "invading" Fort Greely. (All photos, Roy Craft)*

lishment of a major base there August 30, 1942; first bombing of Japanese-occupied Kiska by planes from Adak September 14, 1942; establishment of a U.S. base at Atka September 20, 1942; American occupation of Amchitka January 12, 1943; first bombing of Kiska from Amchitka base February 21, 1943; American assault on Japanese-held Attu launched May 11, 1943; last Japanese attack crushed on Attu to complete one of World War II's most bitter battles, May 29, 1943; occupation of Attu completed May 30, 1943; first raid on Paramushiru July 10, 1943; occupation of Kiska by Allied Forces August 15, 1943.

On Pearl Harbor Day, in the Aleutians, the United States had but two small Army posts and Navy bases. One was on Kodiak Island and the other at Dutch Harbor on Unalaska. In all of Alaska there were but six small Army posts.

When the Japanese attacked Dutch Harbor in June 1942, two secret U.S. airfields had been built flanking Dutch Harbor: one at Cold Bay, the other on Umnak Island. Although typical Aleutian weather blocked a major clash between the Japanese naval forces and the U.S. Eleventh Air Force bombers, the presence of these newly discovered bases probably accounted for the enemy's withdrawal to the west and their occupation of Kiska rather than Dutch Harbor.

Meanwhile, events at Pearl Harbor drastically altered the lives and lifestyles of the military-naval-civilian complex that was Kodiak. Following the attack on American installations and elements of the Pacific fleet in Hawaii, the Japanese, in a propaganda broadcast, had announced the "destruction" of the American base on Kodiak. Although those on the island knew better, men were worried about the effect of the news on their folks at home. Communication with the mainland was difficult if not impossible, and several days of tension followed.

Both naval and military authorities began immediate plans to evacuate dependents of personnel attached to or working on the base. Commander Perry, in a December 7 memorandum, issued the following directive:

"In order to prepare for speedy evacuation to the U.S. it is directed that the small personal luggage and effects necessary for comfort on an ocean voyage be gathered together and placed in readiness for a quick move.

"In case of immediate necessity of evacuation of women and children from the station in the event of an air raid, it is directed that all non-combatants including women and children will be evacuated southward toward Bells Flats. It is expected that any air raid will be of short duration, therefore the evacuees should dress in warm clothing, footwear which will not slip upon ice, and carry sleeping bags or warm blankets; food for three meals should be carried also."

Marine Lt. Col. C. W. Marter, Security Officer, had a similar directive for workmen living on the S.S. *Yale*:

"In the event of an air raid alarm all men on the S.S. *Yale* will proceed rapidly and in orderly manner to the draw which lies on Old Woman's Mountain directly opposite and uphill of the Contractors Barracks 10, 11 and 12. Men in all the barracks will also proceed to this draw by the same road or by climbing the hill opposite the barracks. Dress warmly. In all cases of planes approaching, lie flat on the ground until danger has passed."

There were no raids on Kodiak but the women dependents and children were returned to the States just prior to Christmas on the transport *U.S. Grant*. The unescorted run was made without incident but back on the island the men waited tensely until word was received that their loved ones had arrived safely. Japanese submarines were known to be in the area.

Throughout Alaska's war period, activity at Kodiak was at a fast pace. As Air Force strength developed, planes flying from mainland Alaska to bases in the Aleutian Chain made Kodiak their regular stopping point, and the air station and fort were rest stops for combat flyers between missions farther west.

The first winter was one of hardship for the soldiers stationed at Fort Greely. Although naval air station construction was well along, thanks to an earlier start, the 10,000 soldiers spent their first winter in pyramidal tents heated by Sibley stoves. The winter of 1941-42 has been described by one veteran as an "open winter," meaning it alternated between freezing rains and periodic snows. Mud was deep and the winds were strong. It was uncomfortable. The second winter was better. The

Above — *Partly tame bald eagles were common props for construction workers and servicemen who enjoyed having their pictures taken for the folks back home with the national bird.* Below — *A rare, bronze-covered Bible, a gift from the Czar of Russia to the Russian Orthodox church in Kodiak, held by Father Gleboff for nurse Pauline Browder, from Fort Greely. (Both photos, Roy Craft)*

ground was frozen early and the snow and ice made for easier footing. By that time, warm barracks had been constructed and Fort Greely had become a cantonment rather than a camp-out.

General Corlett, who subsequently commanded the joint Canadian-American expedition to Kiska, the 7th Infantry Division in the Battle of Kwajalein, and the XIX Corps of the First Army in the invasion of Europe, enjoyed a unique rapport with his men. He believed that loyalty starts at the top, and he directed that when materials were available, the first military clubhouse to be built would be for the enlisted men; the second would be an NCO club; and the last an officers' club.

Radio was the principle news medium in Alaska, but few soldiers and others on the island had sets capable of picking up broadcasts from Seattle and other West Coast cities. J. C. "Jack" Henry, Siems-Drake Puget Sound construction superintendent, donated a 15-watt transmitter and a building to house it. The studio was named in his honor. The station went on the air as KODK at noon on New Year's Day, 1942. A federal license had not yet been received, but KODK ignored that. Throughout the area, everyone was encouraged to buy inexpensive radio sets and the station offered a steady diet of recordings, live broadcasts and, best of all, relays of Stateside news programs received by shortwave.

With 10,000 men to draw from, there was plenty of talent and KODK offered entertainment as well as serious news and commentary. There were two military-naval newspapers.

The Kodiak Bear, published at Fort Greely, made its first appearance in early December 1941 and the first two issues were handset in the *Kodiak Mirror* plant. Later, the copy was prepared and flown to Anchorage and professionally printed. It was a full-size newspaper, usually four pages but sometimes six or eight, and it had a circulation of 10,000, largest of any newspaper in Alaska at that time. Copies were distributed to every man on the base and they were encouraged to mail them home. Always light-hearted, the paper was widely quoted in the States and excerpts were frequently featured in *Life* magazine and other publications. At that stage of the war, *The Kodiak Bear* was probably the most famous military newspaper.

Equally bright was the *Willawas*, published by the naval air station and named for the mad, swirling winds for which the Aleutians are noted. Lacking the financing of the larger Army paper, the *Willawas* was mimeographed on yellow paper and maintained a friendly feud with the *Bear*, despite the fact that the staffs and contributors worked closely together.

Much of Kodiak's exposure to the outside world can be attributed to these two newspapers. News correspondents assigned to Alaska found themselves handicapped by strict censorship at the Alaska Defense Command level, but the Kodiak papers were mailed home without restriction and were eagerly quoted by mainland news outlets.

The Kodiak Bear's managing editor was Captain Roy Craft, newspaperman and aide to General Corlett, and its first editor was Private Gene Newhall, University of Minnesota graduate. Its second editor was Private Max Skelton, former editor of the University of Texas's *Daily Texan*. Both Newhall and Skelton later were commissioned and following World War II returned to newspaper careers.

The *Willawas*' first editor was Edward Mannion, ex-newspaperman who later served in the Army, and its second editor was Larry Mathae, who maintained the paper's basic frivolity.

As with the radio station, principal mission of the newspapers was to maintain a high morale among military and naval personnel as well as civilian workmen.

Kodiak was booming. Several nightspots had been added and whenever a ship came in with a cargo of liquor, there were plenty of drinks available, although supplies never lasted long. On military paydays, long lines would form in front of liquor stores and saloons, as well as in a row of structures euphemistically called "houses of ill repute."

Old soldiers said at the time that even if they had to fight another war, World War II and Kodiak would be the one they'd remember. They'll always remember with warmth the hospitality of the downtown community, the occasional roisterous nights, the pleasant times which punctuated the serious days.

—*Roy Craft*

About the Author

In his War Discovers Alaska, 1943 *Joseph Driscoll wrote that* "somehow The Kodiak Bear *is the one paper that stands out and is closely followed by editors back home. Perhaps because the* Bear *is witty, worldly-wise and Rabelaisan. . . . Credit for this can be shared between Major General Corlett, commanding Fort Greely at Kodiak, and his aide-de-camp, Capt. Roy Craft . . . Major General Buckner, chief of the Alaskan Defense Command, praised Corlett as a peerless morale builder, and added:* "The General has a young fellow named Craft on his staff who's a real go-getter and livewire.

"I discovered Craft, erstwhile reporter and rewrite man from Eugene, Oregon, and San Francisco, California, to be all that General Buckner said. He is a pale, undersized fellow who does not sleep well and is forever bursting with ideas to startle and entertain people."

Stranded by the 1964 tsunami, the fishing vessel Albatross *awaits salvage in downtown Kodiak. (All photos these two pages, Guy Powell, Commercial Fish Division, Alaska Department of Fish & Game)*

6

Death from the Sea

One of the most active seismic areas in the world, the Kodiak archipelago is no stranger to calamity. Most dreaded are the earthquakes and giant sea waves called tsunamis. And no one who lived through the rumble which began at 5:36 p.m. Friday, March 27, 1964, will forget it.

It began with a gentle rolling that lasted from 20 seconds to one minute. People waited for it to pass. Instead the tremors increased, the ground rolled like sea waves. Electric power went off everywhere.

Just when some felt the crisis was over, the ocean began to do crazy things: It rolled in an endless sweep

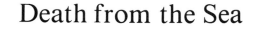

Right — Before and after photos of waterfront businesses, upper, and Kodiak's small-boat harbor, below, show the effects of earthquake-caused tsunamis on the island city.

AFTER

toward shore, ever higher, until the small-boat harbor was filled. Now the waves were over the banks; cars floated or sank. The sea briefly receded and then again swelled to set its course toward the center of town. It flowed over main street, floated frame buildings and trapped people in stores before it went out again.

Once more the water surged, this time shoveling forward everything in its path. Buildings and boats were picked up like match sticks. From Lower Mill Bay Road to Benson was chaos. Wall after wall of water—10 to 12 feet— picked up cannery boilers, crab pots, boats, pilings, logs and boards and hurled them along Mission Road. Thirty homes were thrown into Potatopatch Lake. The Chiniak Road flooded along the south shore of Womens Bay; 3 miles of highway and two bridges were awash. Yards, roads and beaches were strewn with wreckage.

Around the island the tsunamis wiped out the villages of Afognak, Old Harbor and Kaguyak and severely crippled Ouzinkie. Canneries at Ouzinkie and Shearwater were destroyed; Shearwater lost 30 salmon boats; Old Harbor, 20. Every community in the Kodiak archipelago—except Karluk and Akhiok—was damaged. Land subsidence throughout the area was 2 to 6 feet.

Between the southern tip of Kodiak Island and Kayak Island, near Cape Suckling, the waves took 20 lives. Death, near-death and heroism touched everyone. Yule Chaffin's book (*Koniag to King Crab*, 1967) recalls the story of loss to the small village of Kaguyak on the southwestern end of Kodiak Island:

". . .the men of the village council were getting ready to go to a meeting— to discuss—of all things—getting running water for their village. Some of the women had just finished taking steam baths in the banya. Suddenly, someone heard a tidal wave warning on the radio. As the first wave hit, the villagers were already running for high ground.

"After the second wave subsided, the women and children stayed on the hillside while the men went down into the village to get sleeping bags and other supplies. Donald Wyatt and his wife, geologists who were surveying for oil, along with several of the villagers, were trying to get a dory from the beach and take it to higher ground. The third wave caught them. It carried the dory up into a lake. Wyatt, aware that the boat would be sucked back into the bay, pushed his wife out of the boat. Walter Cohen lost his balance and fell out. Simmy Alexandroff, Chief of the village and father of three children, then abandoned his position of safety in an effort to save the others. Mrs. Wyatt and Cohen were helped to safety, but the raging waters took the lives of Mr. Wyatt, Nick Zeedar and Simmy Alexandroff. . . . About daylight, the villagers were taken from their totally destroyed village by rubber life raft. The 60 some villagers of Kaguyak had lost their homes and all possessions. Kaguyak was gone forever, and with it, their brave Chief."

Losses in the archipelago were set at more than $45 million. In total, the violent incoming and outgoing waves destroyed more than 215 structures.

For the then new king crab industry, the natural disaster was a severe blow. A University of Alaska follow-up bulletin (May 1964) from the Institute of Business, Economic and Government Research reported: "The king crab fishing season had begun prior to the earthquake and the value of fishing vessels lost amounted to about $7 million. Other property damage to the industry included the loss of three of four canneries in Kodiak and the destruction of cold-storage plants and associated dock facilities swelled the total loss to over $20 million. . . . Approximately 225 vessels. . .were lost or damaged. Almost all of this destruction was restricted to vessels operating in the king crab industry."

In June, another University of Alaska bulletin said, "Kodiak Island, the hardest hit rural area in Alaska, sustained agricultural damage estimated at $281,000. Losses included the destruction of 35 miles of fences, the death of 200 head of livestock and the ruin of 370 acres of cropland."

The quake had begun in the late afternoon of a widely observed holiday— Good Friday—when schools and most offices were closed.

Kodiak Postmaster Bill Lamme later reported he was "just checking out when the earthquake struck. Clerks ran out the back but my wife, Lillian, and the clerk Ruth were up front. We started back as poles and fluorescent fixtures set up a terrible racket.

"When lights fell on us we huddled

Above — *The earthquake dropped some areas of Kodiak several feet, moving the tidal margin into new areas.* Below — *Litter of destroyed businesses in downtown.*

Most of the Kodiak-based fishing fleet sustained extensive damage during the 1964 disaster. (All photos, Guy Powell, Commercial Fish Division, ADF&G)

between two cabinets instead, and rode the quake out. The concrete floor rolled under our feet. We had not known that an evacuation warning had been given as there was no power. As we started uptown we met a mass of cars and people running out of town for higher ground and learned a tidal wave was expected. We drove to our home atop the hill overlooking the boat harbor and watched from the window. The first wave came in a half-hour and the second at 8 o'clock. The post office is on high ground although several businesses were lost from the same block. Our office backyard is a maelstrom of bunkhouses, boats and buildings.''

As many residents remember, a number of smaller earthquakes followed the big one (registering 8.4 to 8.5 on the Richter scale) and vibrations occurred for many months.

Lamme wrote: "As I type this a coffin is passing in a station wagon, a reminder that life and death go on.''

Sea ice, a winter peril to Kodiak fishermen, coats a derelict on an island beach. (Gerry Atwell, USF&WS)

Weather: Inconstant Constant

Somehow those descriptions of Kodiak Island weather as generally cool and damp with many days of cloud-covered skies do not say it loud enough. Those mild winters you read about are cold and fierce gales *do* lash the islands with monotonous regularity, "mild" winter or "cool" summer.

A visitor's friend once told her it could reach 70° here in summer. After some weeks—repacking her bikini and coconut oil—she said, "Sure, but first it has to reach 60°!"

While reserving "the gloomiest corner of the world" title for "Sitkha," the Russian Khlebnikov described the climate of "Kadiak" as little different: "Clear weather sometimes lasts longer with less change than on Sitkha, but in general the prevailing weather is damp, equally bad for building. Sometimes before December it thaws, with rain; winter begins in January and continues until the middle of March; the first

35

Exposed, rusting ship spikes stand as gravestones above a vegetative mat that now covers most of a vessel's remains. (Guy Powell, Commercial Fish Division, ADF&G)

snow falls on the mountains in early October, the hard frost reaches 15 [degrees] Reaumur [-19° C]. In March and April snow rarely falls and it is very cold; snow lies in the mountains until July; in summer there are more clear days than at Sitkha, but sometimes it is just the opposite; in the summer of 1826 there was so much severe weather that they could not prepare enough iukola and hay. . . ." (Fedorova, *The Russian Population in Alaska and California*, 1973.)

What "transforms the whole region from what would otherwise be inhospitable into a habitation fit for man," wrote Bancroft (*History of Alaska, 1886*), is "the warm Japan current which comes up along the coast of Asia, bathing the islands of the Aleutian archipelago as it crosses the Pacific and washing the shores of America to the southward. It is striking of this warm current of air and water against the cold shores of the North that causes nature to steam up in thick fogs and dripping moistures, and compels the surcharged clouds to drop their torrents."

The average summer maximum temperatures occur in July or August and are in the high fifties and low sixties. Coldest average winter minimum temperatures are in the low twenties in December. Though the average variation from winter to summer is a mere 25°, the record low of -12° F and record high of 86° F indicate periodic influences from the Alaska mainland.

Throughout the year, clouds obscure an average of 70% of the sky at Kodiak. It is completely overcast less than half of the time. Reduced visibility is most persistent and obstructive from June through September when the air contains the most moisture and it is warmer than the ocean. Other conditions that obstruct visibility are rain, drizzle, freezing rain, snow, sleet, smoke and blowing snow.

The normal annual precipitation (liquid form) is over 56 inches but varies from 40 to 80 inches. An average of some 90 inches of snowfall occurs each year, beginning as early as October, but here again varies greatly, 15.9 inches in 1945 to 178.1 inches in 1956.

February is the month with the highest storm frequency. Although the prevailing wind direction is northwest every month except May, June and July—the average speed is about 10 knots—this also can be misleading because of the extreme variability in both direction and speed. Gusts of more than 50 knots have occurred in each month of the year but are most likely in winter. Such storms occur, on the average, about eight times a year.

Sustained, extreme wind speeds at weather reporting stations range from 50 to 70 knots with gusts as high as 100 knots. Wind speeds over water are stronger and, in the event of an unusually intense storm, a sustained wind of about 100 knots is not uncommon.

In winter, Mother Nature is always there to get you at sea with hurricane-force winds, seas masthead high or higher, temperatures 25° below zero with consequent heavy icing and sea water so cold that the strongest man can live in it 5 minutes at most.

"I have my own vision of hell," says former fisherman Tom Casey. "It's a pitching deck, with frozen spray blowing through you, and a hundred-pound halibut on every hook of the line."

Vessel navigation is extremely hazardous in parts of the offshore area, especially around islands where there are many reefs and skerries. Most of the nearshore areas are poorly charted, and much of the offshore area is only lightly charted.

A fisherman says, "Weather is tough. It is the hardest country in the world to forecast. Weather forecasts generalize weather for the area but give no geographic exceptions. For example, you have a westerly wind of 20 to 30 knots in the Shelikof Strait. This same weather pattern generates much higher wind velocities in the Barren Islands area, Port Gore and the Shuyak Island areas."

"I never listen to it [the weather forecast]," another fisherman says. "Every area is so different. There is no way to forecast weather for this island. I use my own barometer and experience."

The generally poor weather conditions make flying extremely hazardous. Most places level enough for landing strips are surrounded by ragged mountains. Everyone seems to have a "worst flight I ever made into (or out of) Kodiak" story and Joseph Driscoll (*War Discovers Alaska*, 1943) was no exception.

He flew to Kodiak in an aged plane, over open water, at 90 miles per hour.

Far left — *Ice crystals on beach grass catch the rays of a setting sun.* Left — *Sea-caused erosion produces caves along portions of Kodiak's beach.* (Both photos, Gary Dobos) Lower left — *Snow, part of an annual average of 90 inches, blankets the small-boat harbor.* (Gerry Atwell, USF&WS)

"In all the years I've been flying," he said, "I've never had crazier trips than the ones out to Kodiak and back, in an antique tri-motor Ford. My first plane ride was taken in one of the Fords, when they were brought on the market in the 20s, and I never dreamed I'd be in one of them again, in the year 1942. . . . Flying out from Anchorage on Sunday, we had to turn back at the halfway point of Homer when the Gulf of Alaska and Shelikof Strait set up a solid barrier of fog."

Chet and Bud Browne, alternate pilots of the Ford on the Kodiak-Anchorage run, had a lanky six-foot-six Texas cowboy for a copilot. Gesturing at the menacing fog, the Texan summed up the perils of Alaska flying when he drawled:

"Weather like this makes you wish you were back home in Texas, sitting safe on a pony."

—Nancy Freeman

"Such Emerald Heights, Such Flowery Vales"

Spring seems to be skipped over some years but the burst of color that proclaims summer is only too welcome on these islands.

Characterized by rocky cliffs and steep slopes, nearly all of the western gulf coastline is covered with some form of grasses or shrubs. Nearest the coast is found grass, *Elymus arenarius*, sometimes called wild rye grass, in sand along the beaches or sometimes on inland dunes. Commonly found nearby are *Senecio pseudo-arnica*, a yellow flower that resembles a daisy; *Lathyrus maritimus*, a beach pea; *Honckenya peploides*, seabeach sandwort; and *Mertensia maritima*, the common oysterleaf. Dominant plant in rockier portions of the coast is *Potentilla villosa*, cinquefoil, which grows in pockets of soil formed in rock crevices.

Further inland the grasses are dominated by bluejoint or *Calamagrostis* group. Two other grasses—the *Poa*,

Far left — *Wild flowers add splashes of color to stands of native grasses along the coast of Shuyak Island, northernmost large island in the Kodiak archipelago. (Gary Dobos)* Left — *Pink-spiked fireweed grows in open areas throughout the island chain. (W.E. Donaldson)*

39

blue grass, and the *Bromus*, brome grass—share the inshore habitat. Even further inland is a mosaic of alpine heath and meadow dominated by *Carex*, or sedge.

The tall vegetation of most of Kodiak Island is composed of birch, *Betula nana*; willow, *Salix*, sp; and alder, *Alnus crispa*. On Afognak, Shuyak and neighboring islands and on the northeast end of Kodiak Island—especially in the vicinity of Spruce Cape and Cape Chiniak—there are dense forests of mature Sitka spruce, *Picea stichensis*.

The low protected valleys of central and eastern Kodiak Island, which are exposed to winds, as well as most of western Kodiak Island and adjacent islands are treeless. Most treeless areas support a thick cover of grass, although low brush and tundra vegetation such as mosses and lichens prevail in some spots.

Besides the forest, brush and open tundra, many species of wild flowers flourish here. Over the years, botanists have noted 40 families of flowering plants that total over 200 different species. The variety is quite spectacular: plants like salmonberry, blueberry, elderberry, highbush cranberry, dogwood, wild rose and devil's club. On the perimeter of the spruce forest are grasses (primarily redtop) and flowers such as lupines, squaw lilies, shooting stars, wild geraniums and various shrubs. Among the smaller flowers are blue or yellow violets, creamy anemones, wild purple irises, bluebells, white or blue Jacob's ladders, daisies, forget-me-nots and hyacinths.

40

Moss-covered branches of a Sitka spruce attest to Kodiak's more than 60 inches of annual rainfall and cool climate. (Gary Dobos)

Thickets of wild roses dot bogs, woods and roadsides. The seed pods, rose hips, are edible and rich in vitamin C. (Carl Bach)

When John Burroughs (a member of the Harriman Expedition from New York) visited Kodiak in 1899 he found Pillar Mountain an "emerald billow" that from the ship looked "smooth as a meadow." Once on shore, however, "the climber soon found himself knee-deep in ferns, grasses and a score of flowering plants, and now and then pushing through a patch of alders as high as his head. He could not go far before his hand would be full of flowers, blue predominating. The wild geranium here is light blue and it tinged the slopes as daisies and butter-cups do at home.

"Near the summit were patches of the most exquisite forget-me-not of a pure delicate blue with a yellow center. . . . Here, too, was a delicate lady's slipper, pale yellow striped with maroon. Here also was a dwarf rhododendron, its large purple flowers sitting upon moss and lichen. The climber also waded through patches of lupine, and put his feet upon bluebells, Jacob's ladder, iris, saxifrage, cassippe and many others. . . ."

Moved to poetry, Burroughs wrote, "Kodiak I think won a place in the heart of all of us. Our spirits probably touched the highest point here. If we had other days that were epic, these days were lyric. I feel as if I wanted to go back to Kodiak, almost as if I could return there to live. So secluded, so remote, so peaceful; such a mingling of the domestic, the pastoral, the sylvan, with the wild and the rugged; such emerald heights, such flowery vales, such blue arms and recesses of the sea, and such a vast green solitude stretching away to the west, and to the north and to the south. Bewitching Kodiak! The spell of thy summer freshness and placidity is still upon me."

41

9

Kodiak's Wildlife

The best-known mammal of these storm-swept islands is an indigenous species, the Kodiak brown bear. A stronghold of the famous bear is the Kodiak National Wildlife Refuge (see that section, page 48) that covers about 82% of the Kodiak Island land mass. Highest bear densities are found on the southern and western parts of the wildlife refuge, although the whole island is bear habitat. These bears inhabit all of the major islands in the Kodiak group and apparently their current distribution differs little, if any, from that prior to the appearance of the Russian settlers.

The northern part of Kodiak Island, where most of the introduced cattle have been kept, is prime brown bear habitat. Studies have shown that bears definitely kill cattle, but game managers strongly resist any move to totally eliminate bears from the area.

Recent estimates of bear populations on the Kodiak National Wildlife Refuge

*A Kodiak bear forages for food in early June.
(Gerry Atwell, USF&WS)*

Top — *Extensive colonies of sea otters, present at Russian occupation, were harvested to the point of extinction. Under federal protection since the turn of the century, the gregarious animals are staging a steady comeback. They are now common to Kodiak's waters. (Gary Dobos)* Above — *Sea lions at Cape Chiniak on Kodiak's outer shore. (Randy Weisser, reprinted from* ALASKA® *magazine)*

Top — *Water spills through a broken beaver dam on Afognak Island. (Daniel H. Wieczorek)* Above — *Seals on Tugidak Island, one of the Trinity group south of Kodiak Island. Tugidak has large seal rookeries and has been the site of extensive commercial seal hunting. (Gary Dobos)*

show approximately 2,000 bears. Projecting this density to the rest of Game Management Unit 8 (Kodiak, Afognak, Chirikof, Semidi Islands and smaller adjacent offshore islands) there are probably 2,500 to 3,000 bears. Afognak Island supports the area's second-largest bear population.

There are other less publicized, but locally popular, game species harvested in the area. For example:

Deer are the most actively hunted big game species in the Kodiak-Afognak Islands complex. A 5-month season and liberal bag limits provide ample hunting opportunity for deer hunters. Depending on population levels, as many as 2,000 Kodiak deer hunters annually harvest 600 to 2,000 deer.

Efforts to transplant Sitka blacktail deer to the Kodiak area began in 1924 with the release of 14 animals on Long Island. Two more deer were released there in 1930 but failure of the deer to move to Kodiak Island prompted the release of nine deer on Kodiak Island in 1934. These introduced animals rapidly expanded into the northeastern corner of Kodiak Island and to adjacent small islands.

The first hunting season was in 1953. By the early 1960's the general southward and westward movement of the deer population had reached Uganik Island area. In the late 1960's deer began to build up in the Uyak, Zachar and Spiridon Bay areas and those areas presently have the highest deer populations on Kodiak and Afognak Islands.

On the eastern side of Kodiak Island, the Shearwater peninsula between Ugak

43

and Kiliuda bays has relatively high deer populations. Raspberry, Shuyak and Afognak Islands' deer populations became well established in the late sixties.

Roosevelt elk occur only in the northern Kodiak archipelago on Afognak Island and nearby Raspberry Island. Eight Roosevelt elk calves were transplanted near Afognak (Litnik) Bay on Afognak Island in the spring of 1929. By 1948 there were about 212 animals. In 1958 there were five major herds with 80% of the animals inhabiting Raspberry Island and the southwest corner of Afognak Island. By 1965 the population peaked at an estimated 1,200 to 1,500 animals.

A decline began in the late sixties; heavy snow accumulations and unusually low temperatures during the winters of 1970 and 1971 caused a massive natural die-off and by 1972 only 450 animals remained. The largest herd now occupies the eastern part of Afognak Island in the Tonki Cape Peninsula area. Herds in the southwest part of Afognak Island and Raspberry Island are still at low levels. But the total elk population appears to be gradually increasing and in 1975 was estimated at about 500 animals.

During 25 years of hunting, more than 1,500 elk have been harvested. When the population was at its highest, hunting was relatively successful. Harvests from 1971 through 1975, however, have averaged less than 25 elk annually and hunter success has been less than 15%. Hunting efforts from 1971 through 1974 averaged only 134 hunters afield annually. More than half the harvest usually is taken during September and October when access by floatplane and small boat is best. After mid-November, hunters use commercial fishing boats and hunt in the coastal areas with limited success.

Southwestern Alaska's only mountain goat population occurs on Kodiak Island. Eighteen mountain goats were introduced at Hidden Basin on Kodiak Island in 1952-53. Since then the population has increased slowly and is now estimated at 150 to 200 animals. Goats occur throughout much of the higher mountainous terrain, although many areas are sparsely populated. Highest concentrations occur in the Hidden Basin creek and Wild Creek drainages.

As a recent arrival on Kodiak, the mountain goat attracts considerable attention from local outdoorsmen who now have an opportunity to hunt the species for the first time. Hunting by permit has been allowed each year since 1968. Annual harvest averages about 10 goats, although 16 goats were taken in 1974. Annual hunter success has averaged more than 50%. Although as many as 66 permits have been issued during the 2-month season, seldom do more than half the hunters actually get into the field.

Weather largely determines actual hunting pressure. Most of the hunting has been concentrated in the Crown Mountain area. Most hunters use float-equipped aircraft for transportation to either Terror Lake or Hidden Basin. Some hunters drive to Saltery Cove and take skiffs to Hidden Basin.

Chiniak Bay on Kodiak Island is used by several thousand sea lions throughout the year. Up to 75 may be hauled out at Long Island and 775 at Cape Chiniak. In the past, small numbers may have been taken for domestic purposes, bait or animal food, or in conjunction with conflicts with fisheries. No commercial harvest has been conducted in Chiniak Bay; however, a total of 14,180 pups were commercially harvested from Marmot Island between 1963 and 1972, years prior to passage of the federal Marine Mammals Act.

The Long Island and Cape Chiniak hauling areas are accessible to recreational boaters from Kodiak and provide good viewing and photographic opportunities.

When white men arrived in the 1740's, sea otters were distributed along most of the coast of southwestern Alaska. Commercial hunting between 1742 and 1911 eliminated the sea otter from parts of the range and greatly reduced numbers in all other areas. In 1911 only small scattered groups of otters were left. Suspected locations of surviving groups include Augustine Island, the Barren Islands, Shuyak Island, northern Unimak Island, Tigalda Island, Samalga Island and several locations in the Andreanof, Delarof and Rat Islands. Some of these nucleus populations have now increased to tens of thousands of animals.

The estimated population of sea otters in the Kodiak archipelago is 4,000 to 6,000 with near carrying capacity around the Barren, Shuyak and northern Afognak Islands and lesser concen-

Top — Red fox pelts, part of the trappers' annual take on Kodiak, are being checked for quality. (Nancy Kemp)
Above — Mountain goats, an introduced species on the island, seek a patch of snow to gain relief from annoying insects and summer heat. (Ed Wickersham)

Top — A Sitka blacktail buck near the ocean's shore. (Gary Dobos)
Above — A goat caught in the act of "dusting," pawing cool, damp soil over its coat. (Ed Wickersham)

trations around the Trinity and Chirikof Islands. There are increasing numbers in an expanding range around southern Afognak and northern Kodiak Islands.

While many areas in the region provide excellent opportunity for viewing and photographing sea otters, much of the area where they are common is inaccessible.

Along rocky coasts land-breeding harbor seals (Phoca vitulina richardii) tend to be scattered, although up to 300 might be seen hauled out in certain prime areas. Larger concentrations frequently occur in glacial fjords, estuaries or near extensive shallow areas where thousands may haul out on glacial ice or sandy beaches. Tugidak Island is a popular haul-out area for the seals.

A conservative estimate, based on aerial surveys and harvest records, reports 270,000 harbor seals in Alaskan waters. The federal Marine Mammal Act of 1972 effectively terminated commercial hunting but viewing and photography of seals has become popular in recent years.

Land otter, weasel and red fox are indigenous to the Kodiak Island archipelago. Beaver were introduced to Kodiak Island and to Raspberry Island in 1924 and are well established on Kodiak, Afognak, Raspberry and Shuyak Islands. Muskrats were transplanted to Kodiak, Afognak and adjacent islands in 1925. Muskrats are abundant near the town of Kodiak.

Marten were released on Afognak Island in 1952 and are well distributed

Top — *A minke whale, smallest of the baleen whales, leaps clear of the water in Ugak Bay. (Daniel H. Wieczorek)* Above — *A red fox dozes in the warmth of midday sun. (Gary Dobos)*

Upper right — *Young harbor seal on the beach at Tugidak Island. (Gary Dobos)* Right — *A short-tailed weasel views the world from under a fishing float. (Carl Bach)*

over the island. Red squirrels, also introduced on Afognak in 1952 as a food source for marten, are now abundant over much of Afognak and Raspberry Islands. Red squirrels were also introduced to the Chiniak area on Kodiak Island. Parka squirrels are found near the town of Kodiak and on some of the smaller islands in the archipelago.

Land otter are abundant over most of the islands in the Kodiak Island group with the exception of Shuyak and Tugidak Islands. Many of the smaller offshore islands have remnant fox populations from fox-farming operations during the early part of the century. Most trapping for fox and otter is from mid-November to early March, and many trappers make sets for both fox and otter. The more successful trappers, using small fishing boats or skiffs for transportation, trap near the beaches. Most trapping is done along the northern two-thirds of Kodiak Island and southern Afognak Island.

Kodiak otters are rated very highly by fur dealers and prices paid to trappers do not fluctuate greatly. Annual harvest is estimated at about 200 to 250 otters, many of which are sold or bartered locally. Trapper export reports on fox indicate that around 200 foxes are sold from Unit 8 annually. The actual harvest is probably near 500 animals in peak years.

The best beaver populations are found on Kodiak Island. Beaver trapping is sporadic; sealing records indicate an average annual take near 200 animals. Trappers begin taking beaver as early as November and frequently trap until the season ends in May.

Rock and willow ptarmigan occur on the major islands in the Kodiak Island archipelago, with the highest numbers in the southwestern part of Kodiak Island. Ptarmigan are hunted near villages and along the Kodiak road system. During early fall a few hunting parties travel by air to the southwestern part of Kodiak Island to hunt ptarmigan. Upper Station Lakes and Tugidak Island are among the most popular hunting areas. Snow machine use for winter ptarmigan hunting has increased in recent years. Total annual harvest in Unit 8 is estimated at 2,000 to 2,500 ptarmigan.

Snowshoe hares were introduced to Afognak and Kodiak Islands with a transplant of 558 animals in 1934. The hares adapted well to the brushy valleys and patchy spruce areas on Kodiak, Long and Woody Islands. Most of the hunting effort for snowshoes occurs near Kodiak along the road system and on Woody Island. Total hunting licenses sales average about 2,000 annually in Kodiak and at least one-third of these people hunt rabbits, but the annual harvest of hares probably does not exceed 3,000.

10

Kodiak National Wildlife Refuge

Kodiak is probably Alaska's best-known island, with its international reputation largely the result of the presence of a mild-mannered but formidable inhabitant—the Kodiak brown bear. Every American's awareness of the fact that these animals still roam the rugged archipelago, of which Kodiak is a part, gives the area a special charm and wilderness mystique.

Prior to the Russians' arrival on Kodiak in the latter 1700's, man and bear shared the island for thousands of years; generally, the bears used the mountains and inland meadowlike expanses of verdure while early man established communities along the coast. These first Kodiakans, Koniag Eskimos, were in harmony with their environment. Their passing left the country virtually unaltered, wild and biologically rich.

Certainly, all life forms that could contribute to this people's existence

48

Winter sun reflects off a placid stream in Kodiak's interior. (Alan C. Paulson)

A hiker pauses on the flank of Barometer Mountain, 2,488 feet, to view Kodiak's interior valleys. (W.E. Donaldson)

were utilized, and bears were no exception; they were killed with special, short, stout arrows. This was done not only for meat and hides but also for the fat, which was melted and served as a drink. Decidedly important in this rain-drenched country was the tough water-proof clothing made from the bears' intestines; the lasting quality surpassed that of similar garments constructed from seal entrails. Bears were held in some esteem, perhaps for their strength, perhaps for their sullen dignity, or perhaps for some ways they enriched the Koniags' lives; the likeness of bear heads has been found decorating stone artifacts.

With contact by modern man, both the Koniags and the bears suddenly became vulnerable to a technology capable of effecting overwhelming and irreversible changes. And both suffered. By the beginning of the 20th century, patterns of land use had markedly changed. By then the Koniags had all but disappeared and commercial enterprises, with heavy demands on the island's resources, replaced subsistence use.

Canneries were built to process

Bears engaging in mock battle along the banks of a salmon stream.
(Gary Dobos)

millions of salmon and fishermen felt that brown bears competed for the fish. Increased numbers of cattle and sheep were introduced and bear-livestock conflicts rose proportionately. Between world wars, when both the livestock and fishing industries became firmly established, local entrepreneurs deeply resented the bears. They called for government hunters to rid the hills of them and some advocated extension of the bounty system to include bears. Meanwhile, hunting seasons and bag limits remained liberal and commercial hunting for hides was both legal and prevalent prior to 1925.

Old-timers recall that as a result, by the early 1930's bear sightings were no longer common. Hrdlicka in his book, *The Anthropology of Kodiak Island*, mentions seeing only one bear while circumnavigating the island close to shore in July of 1932.

By then alarmed, Alaskans joined forces with other Americans to seek permanent sanctuaries for Kodiak's bears. Finally, in 1941, the federal government established the Kodiak National Wildlife Refuge, assuring perpetuation of bears and associated wildlife species. The U.S. Fish & Wildlife Service was directed to administer the refuge, managing it primarily for its wildlife and wild lands. This stewardship also benefits man: photography, fishing, hunting, hiking, rafting and many more activities are allowed in the refuge. Only those actions that would degrade either the wildlife or its habitat are prohibited. Today, refuge lands remain nearly as wild as they were when the Koniags inhabited the islands.

The refuge contains 2,800 square miles of undeveloped country and occupies the southwestern two-thirds of Kodiak Island. Extraordinary in its wild

beauty, it is a unique amalgam of precipitous snow-capped mountains, glacially scoured valleys, rolling tundra, lakes, ponds and streams. Frequent misty and soft summer rains foster lush, verdant growths of heather, grasses, sedges, willows and alders. Fog and clouds often mask the lower elevations, while ragged peaks thrust aloft. Carved by prehistoric glaciers, fjordlike arms of the sea penetrate many miles inland.

A multitude of life forms strive to perpetuate their kind on or adjacent to the refuge. Whales, porpoises and seals frequent the bays. Sea lions congregate along the more isolated and protective rocky sections of the refuge's 800-mile coastline, while many of the islets fringing Kodiak are stippled with colonies of nesting sea birds, such as horned and tufted puffins, black-legged kittiwakes, mew and glaucous-winged gulls and Arctic terns. Two hundred pairs of

Above — Bear tracks point to a winter den near the center of a steep slope. (Gerry Atwell, USF&WS) Left — A quiet stream flowing into Monashka Bay will briefly become a rushing river during the spring thaw. (Jane Elfring)

bald eagles nest on the coast, along rivers or near inland lakes. Brown bears, red foxes, beavers, Sitka blacktail deer and land otters are members of the refuge's mammal community. Rainbow trout, Dolly Varden char, steelhead, and all five Alaska species of Pacific salmon occupy specialized niches in the refuge's extensive river systems. Although salmon runs, with few exceptions, have dwindled from former highs, some streams are still seasonally crowded with silver fish heading for their ancestral spawning grounds. A multimillion-dollar fishing industry relies heavily on salmon as well as shrimp, halibut, and king, tanner, and Dungeness crab stocks, whose existence depends on estuarine habitats in the refuge.

But of all these life forms, it is the brown bear that most excites people's imaginations. These furry titans, about 2,000 of which live on the refuge, are extraordinary creatures. A 1,200- to 1,400-pound male is amazingly agile, whether suddenly whirling to pin a salmon to a stream bottom or relentlessly pursuing a female over extremely precipitous terrain during the breeding season. The females, although much smaller than the males (they rarely exceed 600 pounds), can be aggressive and more than make up for their smaller size if forced to defend their cubs. Few males can withstand the terrible onslaught of an enraged female.

The lives of the bears revolve around the physiological phenomenon of denning: the animals are either readying for it, actually denning or recovering from their 5- to 6-month winter torpor. Dens are dug in November at the upper limits of alder and willow growth. Roots bind the soil, stabilizing walls and roof; branches create wind currents that accumulate deep snow above the den. Beneath this snow the bears are insulated from winter's rigors. During late January or February, females give birth to two or three young, conceived 7 months previously, but held for 5 months in a marvelously complex state of suspended development called delayed implantation. The cubs are very small when first exposed to the den's microclimate, grossing a pound or less. Humans increase their weight 20 to 30 times from birth to maximum growth; a brown bear's weight will increase 600- to 1,400-fold.

In late April and May bears emerge from their winter quarters. Initially

Right — *A nest of alder branches constructed by a bear.*
Below right — *A 4-year-old brown bear well up in a cottonwood tree near Karluk Lake. Folklore maintains that brown bears "never" climb trees. (Both photos, Gerry Atwell, USF&WS)* Below — *An isolated cabin in alpine country near the South Arm Uganik Bay. (W.E. Donaldson)*

they continue to draw sustenance from the still-ample stores of fat accumulated the previous fall and occasionally supplement this energy source with desiccated crowberries from wind-swept ridges. Beginning in mid-May through mid-July bears mate.

The females breed at 4 years, give birth to their first litter at 5, and produce litters at 3-year intervals thereafter. The young stay with the sow for two summers. Although brown bears have lived 30 years in captivity, few attain the age of 20 on Kodiak Island. Females that live this long may contribute a dozen cubs to the population.

When the spring's new vegetation pushes up and color creeps back into the land, the bears move to lower elevations. By late July sufficient salmon will have arrived to attract bears to the streams. Soon the lush growth of grass adjacent to the streams is trampled flat.

During this period not all bears remain along the salmon streams; some trek to alpine areas and feed on nutrient-charged shoots of emerging plants, grazing back and forth on the steep, south-facing slopes where the vegetation occurs in lush stands. In the mountains above the brush line, the bears' activities are easily observed. Rest and play occupy periods between feedings.

Following a rest or brief nap, bears often turn to play. They commonly slide down hard-packed mountainside snowfields and perform a variety of buffoonish antics. For example, once a particularly zany bear was seen sliding on its back down a 50-degree slope while holding a 6- to 8-pound rock pressed to the top of its head with both front paws. Another time a frolicsome animal was jauntily strolling along a knoll when apparently it was smitten by a wave of euphoria: It broke into a lope down a slight incline and, periodically using alternate forepaws as it ran, tore up huge grass-covered clods of earth and flung them arching sideways into the air. This display abruptly ended with a somersault. The bear got up and began to placidly feed.

Bears foraging in alpine areas join their kin along the salmon streams in early August. Berries, high in sugar content, are staples in September and October, but salmon occasionally are used into November.

In preparation for denning, adult bears add 2 to 4 pounds of fat per day for several weeks; the fat becomes 5 or 6 inches thick on the bear's rump. Once the den is excavated, a bear usually remains in the vicinity, loafing in or near the entrance, until entering it to stay sometime in November, when the appropriate mix of weather and body chemistry pushes the animal into its winter lethargy.

The mountains that house these dens have not changed; the lowlands, too, remain essentially wild; protected yet utilized, enjoyed and appreciated. Because of decisive action taken 35 years ago, a largely unaltered land mass exists where a man from New Jersey can come to photograph eagles, or a village housewife can pick berries; a land that supplies trophy bears for the hunter, and deer and bears as winter food for the villagers; a land that provides sport fishing for steelhead and king salmon for the schoolteacher in Kodiak and the insurance salesman from Phoenix. The refuge is a land that is known worldwide for magnificent bears that reign supreme in an unbroken wilderness where man is an infrequent intruder.

But winds of change buffet the refuge. The Alaska Native Claims Settlement Act of 1971 will have far-reaching consequences on landownership patterns in the refuge. Much of the prime wildlife habitat is destined to pass into private hands but, under the act, it will remain subject to refuge rules and regulations. If the natural resources of the withdrawn land are to be perpetuated, yet exploited by the Native landowners in a way that will not conflict with refuge objectives, a close, cooperative working relationship between the villagers and the Fish and Wildlife Service will be necessary. Since most villagers want to maintain their current lifestyles, close cooperation should allow Kodiak to remain just as wild and just as biologically rich as it was under the Koniags.

—Gerry Atwell
REFUGE MANAGER
KODIAK NATIONAL WILDLIFE REFUGE

11

Birds of the Archipelago

The first recorded observations and collections of bird life from the Kodiak Island group date from 1789. In that year the Czar dispatched a Russian ship to the islands to investigate the stories of Russian atrocities perpetrated on the Natives there. The vessel was commanded by an Englishman, Joseph Billings, who, incidental to the main purpose of his voyage, acquired the services of a noted naturalist, Dr. Carl Merck, to gather data and specimens. Merck spent the winter and spring of 1789-90 on Kodiak and sent his accumulated material to St. Petersburg, where it was studied by Peter Simon Pallas. On the basis of these specimens, Pallas produced the first scientific record on Kodiak bird life.

The earliest published references to Kodiak birds known are a few words in Martin Sauer's account of the Billings expedition printed in 1802. "The birds that were observed hereabout were. . .

Northern phalarope, Lobipes lobatus, *a tame, friendly bird that is a fairly common breeder on Kodiak. Phalaropes spend most of the year off the coasts and feed among kelp beds. (W. E. Donaldson)*

wild geese; different kinds of gulls; the crested and tufted auk; blue petrel, of a rusty dark brown, very like the swallow; the foolish and black guillemot divers and a great variety of ducks, the flesh of which are eaten by the natives, the skins used for dresses, and the bills, particularly of the sea parrot, employed for ornament."

Today, nearly two centuries after Merck set foot on Kodiak, much remains to be learned about its birds. Birds, however, have always played an important role in the lives of the people of the area. They were a source of food and dress for the early Natives but, more importantly, pelagic birds play a major role in recycling the ocean's nutrients and directly affect the growth and production of ocean creatures. Sea birds excrete phosphates and nitrates from their diet of marine organisms, elements that are needed to maintain the phytoplankton (minute plants) production of the oceans. Phytoplankton in turn is food for the small fish which are food for larger fish, some of which are the economic backbone of the community.

In addition, today birds are a valuable recreational resource to hunters and bird watchers alike. Waterfowl hunters took 2,500 ducks during the 1974-75 season. The most common duck harvested was green-winged teal.

In all 176 species of birds have been recorded at Kodiak and its adjacent waters. Of these, 90 species are known to breed on the island. The island's proximity to the mainland of Alaska and the surrounding North Pacific

1

1. Old squaws, Clangula hyemalis, *dive for their food, crustaceans and mollusks.*
2. A female red-throated loon, Gavia stellata, *incubating her single egg.*
3. Black-footed albatrosses, Diomedea nigripes, *and fulmars,* Fulmarus glacialis, *the smaller birds, squabble for food tossed from a fishing vessel.*
4. Dunlins, Erolia alpina, *in winter plumage. They are uncommon migrants to the island's tidal flats and freshwater marshes.*
5. The sharp-tailed sandpiper, Erolia acuminata, *is also uncommon on the island. It breeds in northern Siberia and winters as far south as New Zealand.*
6. Rock sandpiper, Erolia ptilocnemis, *in winter plumage. The bird feeds at low tide in the intertidal zone.*
7. The tufted puffin, Luna cirrhata, *is also called a sea parrot.*
8. Short-billed dowitcher, Limnodromus griseus, *a species common to Kodiak's marsh areas in the summertime.*
9. Black oystercatcher, Haematopus bachmani, *feeds on bivalves in the intertidal zone. (All photos, W. E. Donaldson)*

2

5

3

6

4

7

8

9

1. *Black-billed magpies,* Pica pica, *are abundant on Kodiak.*
2. *The common redpoll,* Acanthis falmmea, *flocks up during the winter months and is frequently seen at feeders in the town of Kodiak.*
3. *The golden-crowned sparrow,* Zonotrichia atricapilla, *is present in large numbers during the summer.*
4. *Downy woodpecker,* Dendrocopos pubescens, *the smallest woodpecker found in Alaska, is a common resident of Kodiak. It favors willow-alder complexes where it feeds on insects, their eggs, and grubs.*
5. *White-winged crossbills,* Loxia leucoptera, *feed on spruce-cone seeds.*
6. *Northern three-toed woodpecker,* Picoides tridactylus; *uncommon on the island.*
7. *Red-faced cormorants,* Phalacrocorax urile, *common nesters on offshore islands.*
8. *Savannah sparrow,* Passerculus sandwichensis, *an abundant summer visitor and breeder.*
9. *Adult bald eagle,* Haliaeetus leucocephalus, *with the remains of a spawned-out salmon, a chief source of food. (All photos, W. E. Donaldson)*

Ocean contribute to Kodiak's unique blend of land and oceanic birds. There are also frequent casual or accidental visits by North American and Asiatic species that stray from the normal migration routes.

While the main migratory routes bypass Kodiak, spring and fall migrations to the island are still exciting events. Spring migration begins in April with the first arrivals, whistling swans and black brants. Some whistlers nest on the island while the brants briefly rest before heading for the eelgrass beds at Izembek Lagoon on the Alaska Peninsula. Among the first shore bird migrants in the spring are the greater yellowlegs, quickly followed by the black and golden plovers and least sandpipers. Spring migration generally peaks between the end of April and the middle of May and, by then, the island seems to be alive with birds.

The most abundant migrants are the pintail ducks and black brants followed by mallards, green-winged teals and shovelers. Shore birds are represented in numbers by the plovers, greater yellowlegs, surfbirds, turnstones, phalaropes, dunlins, western and least sandpipers, common snipes and tattlers. Small land birds arrive in numbers in early to mid-May and include violet-green, tree and bank swallows; hermit and gray-cheeked thrushes; orange-crowned, yellow and Wilson's warblers; and the sparrows—savannah, golden-crowned, fox and song.

Spring migration time also marks the departure of overwintering birds that have come from harsher more northern climates to the temperate coastal areas of Kodiak the previous winter. Oldsquaws, scaups, goldeneyes, buffleheads, eiders, scoters and elegant emperor geese come to the island to take advantage of the ice-free conditions in many of its bays and estuaries to make a living during the cold winter months. At the first sign of the long northern summer, they assemble with others of their kind for the return flight to their more northern nesting grounds.

The third major event of spring bird movement is the arrival of offshore pelagic birds inshore, close to their nesting islands and cliffs. The first of this movement, the black-legged kittiwake, moves inshore in early April and is a harbinger of spring. Fulmars, horned and tufted puffins also move in by the thousands to claim little pieces of rock for their brief nesting seasons.

The fall migration covers an expanded period of time; birds may begin moving south as early as July or as late as the end of October. The length of a species' incubation and rearing time controls when the bird can depart. Fewer birds pass through at the onset of winter and several species not present in the spring are late-season visitors, such as the sharp-tailed sandpipers. These birds nest in and around Siberia. During fall migration some make their way across the Aleutian Chain through Kodiak and down the west coast of North America. The fall migration period also marks the onset of an offshore movement by the ocean-going birds.

Kodiak Island is home to 56 species of birds that can be found year-round. Many of these, however, abandon summer habitats to congregate in winter around dwindling food supplies in coastal areas. Some frequent the feeders placed out by local residents and others have learned that fishing vessels returning to the harbor often produce free meals. Representatives of this group include black-capped chickadees, nuthatches, varied thrushes, magpies, crows, ravens, pine grosbeaks, bald and golden eagles, glaucous-winged and mew gulls.

Kodiak's bird life offers diverse opportunities for recreationists and naturalists alike.

—Bill Donaldson

Sports Fishing at Kodiak

Unlike most other Alaska waterbound coastal communities, Kodiak Island has a 120-mile road network that, among other things, provides direct access to 20 streams, many miles of sandy-rocky beaches and a score of small lakes and ponds. There's excellent trout and salmon fishing in most of the remote streams and all of the roadside lakes are stocked with either trout, landlocked cohoe salmon or arctic grayling. For anglers who like isolation and wilderness, local air taxi services can also provide transportation to any number of remote fishing areas.

To take advantage of Kodiak's good fishing, anglers must understand the habits of the island's fish. While a Michigan brook or brown trout may be streambound for its entire life, most salmon, trout and char use Pacific streams only briefly, for spawning and short-term rearing. And the precise

Red salmon struggle to overcome Fraser Falls to reach their spawning grounds in western Kodiak. (Gerry Atwell, USF&WS)

up to 1 pound. Unlike the trout they have no tail spots and are, of course, much smaller than salmon. Initial success is usually low but by the first week in May Dolly fishing reaches its height. By then the finny Buskin Lake residents are swarming through the river and more than 10,000 will be caught by the time the seaward migration is completed in early June.

Anglers who fly to lakes, such as Karluk and Uganik also find thousands of char staging their seaward migration in the spring. Fishermen working outlet streams from the lakes will also catch rainbow trout up to 20 inches and steelhead as large as 30 to 35 inches. Another fine area for early char is the Portage Lake outlet on Afognak Island. This 2-mile-long stream also has good fishing for rainbow trout and steelhead. Other area rivers or streams with good May to June trout fishing include Karluk, Red, Ayakulik, Fraser, Afognak, Malina, Barabara, Upper Station, Akalura and Little River.

The Dollies are easily caught on eggs, small spoons, spinners and sparsely tied streamer flies. By the first of June they have left the streams and are prey for anglers fishing along salt-water beaches. Rocky areas where the ocean floor drops off quickly are best.

Subsistence fishermen start catching red salmon in the Buskin Beach area around May 15 but it is usually early June before sports anglers catch reds in the river. (In the Kodiak area all waters with rainbow trout also have runs of reds.) They average 22 to 24 inches long and weigh about 9 pounds. Like Dollies

Above — Some salmon challenge the natural hazards of a falls even though fish ladders, structures at right, have been built on many Kodiak streams to ease the fishes' passage to upstream spawning grounds. Left — A spawned-out dog salmon nearing the end of its life cycle. (Both photos, Gerry Atwell, USF&WS)

timing of salmon and steelhead runs at Kodiak is different from other Pacific coastal areas.

About April 15, when the first real hint of spring is in the air, serious anglers drive from Kodiak 35-plus miles to Pasagshak River to fish for the first Dollies of the season. Sea-run Dolly Varden are actually char (like the brook trout) and most spend their winters in a lake. In the spring they are slender and range up to 26 inches long. Most, however, are 12 to 16 inches and weigh

Sports fisherman with an average-sized silver salmon.
(Gary Dobos)

they have no tail spots. They are heftier and have a bluish color on their back.

A hooked red is a tough customer and fairly stout gear is needed to land it. But there is no harder salmon to hook than a red. The most neatly placed fly or lure will be spurned. They move into the streams with the rising tide and characteristically mill, jump and announce their presence to the anglers. Their fastidious feeding habits and flaunting jumps can be points of frustration for anglers and catching reds involves both persistence and luck. Large streamer flies, medium-sized lures and patience sometimes produce fish.

If your purpose is to catch lots of fish, hold off fishing salmon in the areas near roads until at least July 4. If you can't wait for the salmon, the alternative is to fly to where there are some. June fishing at Karluk Lagoon for king salmon is worth the price of a charter and then some.

Karluk River flows out of Karluk Lake 22 miles before it enters the 3-mile-long Karluk Lagoon. It averages about 200 feet across and is very shallow. It's easy to fish wearing hip boots, but float trips will be interrupted by shallow stream sections that have to be hiked. Many anglers put in at the lake then float, fish and camp along the river down to the lagoon.

A commercial lodge is available for overnight visitors at Karluk village on the lagoon. The village is also reached by scheduled air service. In addition there are Bureau of Sports Fish and Wildlife recreational cabins at Karluk Lake and approximately 8 miles below

Karluk Lake, popularly known as Karluk Portage. Anglers may reach the portage area by flying to the head of Larsen Bay and hiking a scenic trail overland to the river.

Red River (or Ayakulik) is very similar to Karluk but it is more inaccessible. Most anglers arrive by small planes that can land on the beach with wheels during low tides. Access can also be gained by landing on Red Lake and portaging about 3 miles to the main river.

Kings are found in the intertidal areas of both Karluk and Red rivers during early June and are usually caught on lures or eggs attached to stout fishing gear. These fish average about 25 pounds although 30- to 40-pounders are not uncommon. By late June or early July the kings are found in the central river areas and by mid-August they are in spawning condition.

In addition to the seasonal arrival of all species of Pacific salmon, the Red and Karluk rivers contain the largest populations of steelhead available in the Kodiak area. Steelhead arrive in the lagoon areas in late August to early September and fishing for them is excellent from October through freeze-up. Fish caught by spring anglers overwintered in the area and are in a spawning or spawned-out condition.

It's about July 4 when pink salmon or humpies show in the bays flanking Kodiak's road system. They first appear off the beaches near Myrtle and Roslyn creeks and Chiniak Bay on the incoming tides. Bright spoons and spinners are the best lures for taking

Upper left — *All species of Pacific salmon, plus steelhead, rainbow trout, Dolly Varden and grayling, are present in many Kodiak streams. This fisherman tries his luck at Salonie Creek, flowing into Womens Bay southwest of Kodiak. (Frank Van Hulle)* Above — *Sports fisherman with a rainbow. (Gayle Poradek)* Left — *Afognak, the other large island in the archipelago, is also laced with waterways, such as Gretchen Creek, that support sports fisheries. (Frank Van Hulle)*

Right — *Portage Creek on Afognak Island.* Below — *A string of Dolly Varden caught in Buskin River. (Both photos, Frank Van Hulle)*

pinks and hip boots aid anglers in wading to within casting distance of schooled fish. They are great jumpers and can often be located by watching likely bays, creek mouths and schooling areas.

The ocean-bright pinks are sleek and silvery with conspicuous spots on both lobes of the tail. They are excellent fare when fresh from the sea. Upon reaching the streams the sleek form develops a distinctive hump and the silvery sheen turns reddish with brown-green blotches on the sides.

When pinks reach spawning condition they lose most of their food qualities. For this reason most of the roadside streams are closed from August 1 through September 10 in the main spawning areas. The creek mouths and lower portions of the streams remain open to allow anglers to harvest some of the late-running fish. Pinks continue to enter the streams well into August and anglers can find excellent fishing for them in almost any of the roadside bays during this midsummer period. Pinks are fine fighters but many a late August angler has been pleasantly surprised by a fierce strike and a long hard fight from a fish less often caught in the area, the dog or chum salmon.

Chums are big fish that average about 30 inches long and weigh 8 to 15 pounds. They don't strike as readily as pinks. Their large size and the absence of tail spots distinguish them from pinks. When fresh from the sea, chums appear similar to reds. However, dogs are caught later in the year and often have an indistinct mottling on the side.

Once the fish enter fresh water, the mottling becomes very distinct, resembling paint that has run and greenish bars develop along the sides. They are caught in the same manner as pinks and like all Pacific salmon lose most of their food qualities when they enter the spawning cycle. Fresh from the sea, dogs make an excellent canned or smoked fish.

While the timing of the reds, kings, pink and chum salmon is fairly similar throughout the area, cohoe or silver salmon follow a different schedule. By early August large schools of silvers are in the bays fed by major Afognak Island streams. Some of the better areas include Discoverer Bay, the estuary of Portage Creek, Pauls Lake, below the outlet of Laura Lake, the Marka Bay area and the lake area near the outlet of Lily Pond Lake. These waters are accessible only by airplane or boat.

The first cohoes will show up in the Kodiak area later in August but it is usually mid-September before fishing becomes good. Pasagshak River is the first accessible area for early cohoe fishing. They arrive early in this stream and move in and out with the tide. The system supports the largest accessible run for Kodiak anglers and fishing is excellent from late August through September. By mid-September there is good cohoe fishing in almost all of the major streams and along the beach areas. Cohoe average 10 to 12 pounds, are caught on eggs, lures or flies and are excellent fighters.

Pacific halibut commonly move into the immediate offshore water of the Kodiak Island group in late May or early June. Anglers fishing from boats often catch halibut of 50 to 100 pounds but most fish average about 15 pounds. The common method used to catch halibut is to fish relatively flat areas on the ocean floor near kelp beds with either cut herring or large shiny lures for bait. This type of fishing also produces flounder, greenling cod and the unwelcome Irish lord or sculpin.

Black rockfish (sometimes called black bass) are common around the rocky reefs in Monashka Bay and near Spruce Island. These fish commonly move in schools and once located are easily caught. Any type of bright spinner or spoon will catch a rockfish. They are excellent eating and weigh up to 6 pounds.

—*Frank Van Hulle*
SPORT FISH BIOLOGIST
ALASKA DEPARTMENT OF
FISH & GAME, KODIAK

13

Afognak Logging

The Kodiak Western floatplane slid into Kazakof (Danger) Bay on Afognak Island. A playground for Roosevelt elk and Sitka blacktail deer, this second-largest island in the Kodiak group also abounds with bear. Forewarned of "animals the size of trucks, drifting behind the cover of brush," I was sure I could hear them breathing. But it was trees, not bears, that brought me to Afognak Logging Camp, guest of company vice-president Al Schafer.

We landed near the 12 new mobile units for loggers and their families. Placed fan-shaped around the bay in this park setting, the trailers look more like vacation homes for the 23-man crew working practically nonstop, 7 days a week. The push is to get on with the job, under the terms of the Perenosa timber sale, which began with road building in 1975 and continues as the first portion of 12,000 acres of spruce are harvested.

1. Afognak Logging Camp, Kazakof Bay.
2. Road and logging superintendent Bill Baird at the post office.
3. Log bridges protect stream banks, prevent siltation.
4. Leroy Phillips, once a chef at major hotels, prefers logging camps.
5. Grapple yarder handling the first of 332 million board feet cut. (All photos, Nancy Freeman)

A narrow ribbon of road—lacing the island some 23 miles north to south—was completed in May. As the road was constructed, limbs and stumps in the right of way were cleared. Adjacent areas were cleaned, leveled, reseeded. "Is that grass?" "You're darn right it is," exults Schafer, pointing to ditches checkered with new, green growth. The first part of the road is smoother than Mill Bay Road (a main artery in Kodiak) and, when the snow clears (yes, snow still in June) the north end will be rolled, edges tidy.

Along the way, Schafer and Bill Baird, road and logging superintendent, point out the bridges built over streams, which for centuries have burst with red and silver salmon. Logs were placed carefully to avoid disrupting either the banks or the streams. "We didn't even disturb the moss," Baird says.

The country is breath-taking. Some 120,000 acres of moss-draped spruce. The road, Schafer feels, also means "access to a lot of people, so they can see and enjoy it." Here is a sweet-smelling northern jungle and the men and machinery are miniature by comparison.

Down the road Baird stops for a large elk—"that's the biggest cow I've seen," he says—while I scramble out of the pickup for a picture. Unmoved by the commotion, the stately elk continues to stare down the photographer for several seconds before turning tail and melting into the brush.

"Want us to cough up a bear?" Schafer asks. He explains there has

Far left — *Small stands of trees are invading Afognak Island grasslands.* Lower left — *Logs, one of Afognak's major products, ready for shipment to mainland mills. (Both photos, Gordon Edgars, U.S. Forest Service)*

been no confrontation between his men and bears. "No bear has been shot and no man has been mauled. We seem to be coexisting," he says, "and the bears don't seem to be moving out." To the contrary, the loggers have counted seven to eight bears on a stream, gorging on fat silver salmon.

Actual logging started in early June. In the future it is expected to continue year-round, producing a total of 332 million board feet valued at roughly $7 million in stumpage receipts. Selected trees are probably 100 feet, averaging 80 feet from stump to top-cut of usable, "good, No. 2-type lumber." Very little rot is found, convincing the loggers that this timber is prime and being harvested at its peak.

Two large pieces of machinery, like prehistoric monsters, grab the trees with their crab-shaped pinchers and poke them in ever-growing piles. Representing an investment of $600,000, the grapple loader and grapple yarder replace the traditional "choker setter" of earlier days, making it possible to do more work with fewer men.

The U.S. Forest Service engineered the road, laid out boundaries for cutting units and generally controls the sale. But the Kodiak Conservation Society suit, asking the U.S. Forest Service to cancel the sale (and naming Afognak Logging as codefendant), has delayed construction of a sawmill on the island. Logs cut as much as 2 years ago remain stockpiled and, Schafer says, "out of desperation we are forced this year to barge the logs to either Seward or Homer." There is the

Above — Modern trailers are fully equipped and provide logging employees with a homelike atmosphere. (Nancy Freeman) Right — *The natural encroachment of spruce into grassy areas begins the cycle of forest extension. These heavily coned trees in time will create a new forest.* Far right — *A sports fisherman on an Afognak stream. (Both photos, Gordon Edgars, USFS)*

condition of the logs to consider and the fact that "2½ years of the (10-year) sale have elapsed. We can't wait forever for a sawmill." When the situation is right, he says, there will be a mill on Afognak. A $3 million sawmill built especially for the Perenosa timber sale is waiting on a barge in Portland, Oregon.

The Perenosa timber sale will harvest about 6% of Afognak Island timber by 1983. Eleven hundred acres are to be harvested yearly in average cutting units of 100 acres each. To date, the harvest has begun in two units.

Major spruce growth is on the northern and southern ends of the island and is slowly invading the grasslands. The oldest spruce stands, from 350 to 400 years old, cover the northern one-third of the island in a contiguous stand. The southern two-thirds of Afognak contain stands of timber in varying sizes and ages up to 350 years. From this trend, foresters believe that presently unforested areas will also become invaded with spruce. And if cutover areas do not regenerate naturally, the Forest Service will undertake artificial regeneration.

Timber cutting is not new to Afognak. During World War II the U.S. Army logged about 440 acres and had a sawmill near the present camp. Lumber produced there was used for construction on Kodiak and throughout the Aleutians. Then a small sawmill was built at Raspberry Strait by Valley Logging Company in the 1950's. Some 300 acres were logged until 1964 when the mill was destroyed by the earthquake and tidal wave.

Back in camp for cook Leroy Phillip's thick tomato soup and homemade oatmeal cookies, we sat in the sparkling yellow-tiled, shiny aluminum world of the mess hall. There is a small-town atmosphere about the camp, unusually bright and clean for a remote operation. A hand-painted sign on a stick reads: "Arctic survival kit. If lost, put stick in ground. Within 10 minutes a truck driver will show up and run over it." Parked outside is Baird's all-terrain vehicle named after a nearby creek officially dubbed "Fuzzy Bugger Creek" by the U. S. Forest Service. Two trailer "bunkhouses" (one is an 18-man unit; the other can house 20) are spotless and fully equipped. By fall there is to be a D-shaped lawn. There is a central fuel system and locally generated power. The camp has its own communication system, including an in-house radio between Schafer's town office and Danger Bay.

Mechanic foreman Joe Lawton keeps generators, boilers and furnaces running and tends to the 40-odd pieces of big equipment. Other foremen are Ira Shepherd, in charge of the cutting crews, and Ron Rusher who operates Afognak Logging Company's tug, the *Cygnet*, indispensable for carrying supplies and providing emergency transportation.

Saturday is movie night at Danger Bay. Films flown in by Afognak Logging Company are usually ahead of the fare offered by town theaters but one employee remembers a recent exception: a movie so old that Gabby Hayes got the girl.

"We try to give the family men Sunday off," Baird says, while others rotate their trips to Kodiak. Schafer estimates the company has spent more than $4 million through labor and equipment in the Kodiak Island area since 1974. The 1975 payroll was roughly $600,000 and is expected to top $1 million in 1976. The dollars are spread around. Groceries and meat are bought at Kraft's; substantial business goes to Sutliff's and Kodiak Western. "What isn't spent in Kodiak is mostly banked there," Schafer says.

Camp employees, including Forest Service personnel, may reach 60 this year. It has cost Afognak Logging Company time and money to pursue a plan "easiest on the land, but," Schafer says, "we're being doubly careful not to foul up and still get the job done."

It shows.

—*Nancy Freeman*

Afognak's Other Resources

Much is old about Afognak Island but the new is apparent too. Salmon have probably spawned in its streams since before recorded time; only recently has man installed aids for salmon to find their way to new spawning grounds to increase fish populations. Nature, too, has enriched the land; nearby volcanic eruptions have added ash to the soils on Afognak over the past 3,000 to 4,000 years. A more recent natural event are the trees. Foresters believe that the Sitka spruce stands have only been growing on the island over the past 350 years; a very short time in the ways of nature.

Natural history overlaps human history on Afognak Island. Aleuts probably knew the island in its unforested state. By the time European explorers arrived, the forest on Afognak would have only begun to be established.

In U.S. history, Afognak Island was first set aside as public land in 1892 as

A lightweight aluminum fish ladder, the first used in Alaska, installed at Pauls Lake, Afognak Island. (Gordon Edgars, USFS)

Above — *A Malina lakes area recreation cabin, one of four on Afognak maintained by the U.S. Forest Service. (Gordon Edgars, USFS)* Left — *Shaded, damp forest floors stimulate rich growths of moss. (Gary Dobos)*

the Afognak Forest and Fish Culture, under President Benjamin Harrison. In 1908, President Roosevelt consolidated the area into the Chugach National Forest and it has been under U.S. Forest Service management since that time.

Much of Afognak Island will be transferred to private ownership under the Alaska Native Claims Settlement Act of 1971. The process will take several years but future policies will be set by the Native corporations.

Big game animals on Afognak Island are brown bear, Roosevelt elk and Sitka blacktail deer. The elk, found only in Alaska on Afognak Island, and the deer are introduced species that have prospered. Habitat management for these animals is becoming increasingly important and will become more intensive as road access is developed. The island also has a good population of pine marten and beaver.

The Chugach National Forest, in conjunction with the Alaska Department of Fish & Game, has undertaken fisheries habitat improvement projects on Afognak Island. Projects include installation of aluminum fish passes on Portage Creek, Laura Creek, Pauls Lake, Gretchen Lake and Seal Bay. The Alaska Department of Fish & Game also operates a salmon research lab and hatchery at Kitoi Bay.

The U.S. Forest Service maintains four recreation cabins on Afognak Island for public use; these may be reserved at any Forest Service office by paying a fee and obtaining a permit. Recreation cabins are located at Portage Lake, Afognak Lake, Malina lakes area and Waterfall Lake. The cabins are quite popular and heavily used in the summer months. They provide good fishing and hunting opportunities in a wilderness setting. Many lakes and streams contain excellent sport fishing.

Afognak is rich in natural resources. Salmon spawn in its streams, hunters stalk its big game, loggers harvest its trees, thereby enriching the local economy, and photographers record its mysterious beauty. Recreation, wildlife, and timber resources exist on the island with mutual benefit to all. Continued wise use of the land will preserve the beauty and bounty of Afognak Island for generations to come.

—Chris Reichert

Island Villages

Six villages, inhabited primarily by people of Aleut ancestry, are an important part of the Kodiak Island Borough. Between 1960 and 1970 the combined growth rate of Port Lions, Ouzinkie, Old Harbor, Akhiok, Larsen Bay and Karluk was 15%. Their economy is heavily dependent upon the fishing industry, which offers nearly all of the opportunities for employment and cash income.

The communities have relatively modern housing and offer a wider range of facilities and services than are found in most Alaskan villages. Although none of the borough villages has a road connection with Kodiak, all are linked to Kodiak via regularly scheduled air service; and fishing boats are commonly used to transport passengers and goods.

Top right — Port Lions was established after the 1964 earthquake by combining the populations of the old villages of Afognak and Port Wakefield. (Gerry Atwell, USF&WS) Right — Ouzinkie, 10 miles north-northwest of the city of Kodiak. (Betsey Myrick)

Top — *Ouzinkie's post office, center of the 100-plus-population community. (Carl Bach)* Above — *Ouzinkie, like all Kodiak Island communities, relies heavily on commercial fishing. (Nancy Kemp)*

PORT LIONS

A forward-looking community 19 miles west-northwest of Kodiak, Port Lions is a fourth-class city of about 250 people. A new city, Port Lions was formed after the tidal wave of 1964 by the relocation of the villages of Afognak and Port Wakefield (on Afognak Island) to Settler Cove, an arm of Kizhuyak Bay.

There are at least three ways to get to Port Lions from Kodiak: a 2-hour ferry ride departing once a week in winter, twice in summer, for about $5; weather permitting, a 10- to 20-minute scheduled flight, which costs about $15; or a long, three-hour boat trip following the coastline.

Although a fire in 1975 leveled the Wakefield cannery and eliminated the city's main source of employment, Port Lions formed a corporation and purchased a floater that is processing king crab, tanner crab, salmon, halibut and shrimp.

Port Lions has a Russian Orthodox church, lighted streets, phone service, electricity, a fire truck, a 2,500-foot airstrip, community hall, clinic, library, fuel delivery, 8-hour-a-day cable TV service, grocery, cafe, inn and privately owned sawmill.

The elementary school has between 65 and 70 children, recently added 9th grade and may add 10th grade during the 1976-77 school year.

Plans call for upgrading the water and sewer system; and the first sale of city lots in a decade will permit construction of new residences to ease a housing shortage.

Port Lions is quiet, clean and crime free. Dr. Michael Emmick, resident physician, handles once-a-week garbage collection and is the town's only police officer. As keeper of the peace, Emmick grins, "I have a zero record. I've never arrested anyone yet."

OUZINKIE

Author Yule Chaffin has described Ouzinkie as a place "where cars are not needed or wanted and where people may watch from their shores the steamy vapor spouts of whales out in the blue waters of Marmot Bay."

On the west end of Spruce Island, about 10 miles north-northwest of Kodiak, Ouzinkie is easily accessible from town: about a half-hour by skiff or a 10-minute plane ride (weather permitting).

Ouzinkie is a fourth-class city of about 100 to 150 people, most of whom fish or work in fish processing or timber. A small sawmill on Spruce Island, about 2 miles from the village, has operated intermittently, and three village corporations are now planning to establish a specialty mill at Ouzinkie.

The cannery fire here in 1975 more than eliminated a source of income: it also knocked out the system that generated power for part of the town and operated the village's water supply. Townspeople are working to set up adequate electrical generation.

Central to community life is the

Russian Orthodox church, the Baptist Mission, the school and the store. The Russian Orthodox church, located at the south end of Spruce Island at Icon Bay, has been in use almost continuously since the original settlement by the Russians in the late 1700's.

Ouzinkie is a beautiful spot surrounded by hilly and heavily wooded country.

OLD HARBOR

Hospitality is legendary at Old Harbor, a fourth-class city nestled on a ribbon of beach on Sitkalidak Strait, about 53 miles southwest of the city of Kodiak, that was established in 1884.

The first permanent white settlement in Alaska was established 100 years earlier in nearby Three Saints Bay by merchant and fur trader Grigori Shelikov. This site became the main fur trading center for the Russian-American Company. During its brief life span, the first mission and day school in the entire northwest coast of North America was at Three Saints Bay. In 1792 the Russian colony was moved to the present site of the city of Kodiak.

A destructive tidal wave was one reason behind the move of the colony. Another tsunami destroyed the village of Old Harbor in 1964. It has been rebuilt in the same location and today has a population of between 250 and 300.

An admirer says, "Old Harbor is really planning for the future. . .they really have their stuff together." He refers to construction of 45 units of housing; plans for telephones and TV; and eventually community-owned electrical generator and a locally owned seafood processor to replace the *Sonya*, which was gutted by fire in 1975.

Based on a fishing economy, Old Harbor has a church, two stores, a post office, a good airstrip, small-boat harbor and a show house (with pool tables and electronic hockey). Old Harbor is proud of its community hall—Alfred Naumoff Memorial Building—which houses a health clinic, library, village corporation and village council offices and some facilities for overnight guests.

As in all the villages, concern for the children is high in Old Harbor. There is a Head Start program, an elementary school and the beginnings of a high school program. Children and adults are learning the Aleut language and an old coffee shop is being renovated for a day-care center.

"Old Harbor," an agency worker says, "is solving its own problems."

AKHIOK

When a plane lands in the bay and taxis to the edge of the shore at Akhiok, the whole village turns out in greeting. A friendly, hardy community on the southwestern tip of the island, Akhiok is about 91 miles from the city of Kodiak and 38 miles southwest of Old Harbor.

The name Akhiok or Akhiak is believed to be the Russian name for a once-flourishing sea otter hunting village. (U.S. postal authorities briefly

Above — Akhiok is thought to have been the site of a flourishing sea otter hunting village under the Russians. Now the community relies on commercial fishing for its economy. Left — A banya, a Russian steam bath, a fixture in many Kodiak villages. (Both photos, Nancy Kemp)

Left — Old Harbor was rebuilt after the 1964 earthquake and tsunami. (Gerry Atwell, USF&WS)

The Larsen Bay cannery, serving a prolific fishery, has been in operation for more than a half-century. (Gerry Atwell, USF&WS)

changed the name to Alitak during World War I because of its similarity to another Alaskan community, Akiak.) With the decline of the sea otter industry, the Russian-American Company withdrew and many families moved away. Much later, after the 1964 earthquake, some villagers from Kaguyak, whose homes had been destroyed, were relocated to Akhiok. Today, the villagers, 100 or so in the summer and about 75 in winter, fish for salmon or work in the cannery at Alitak, about 15 minutes away by skiff. Some hunt seal on a subsistence basis.

Electricity is intermittent and provided by private generators. The village water and sewage systems also need upgrading. Keeping an adequate supply of stove oil has long been a problem and the village runs out, usually in midwinter. Fuel is held in household drums and families rely on driftwood to keep warm when the oil is gone.

Freight is brought by plane; heavy items by fishing boat. Groceries, ordered from Kodiak and delivered by aircraft to be resold through a co-op store, are expensive.

During low tide, planes may taxi up onto the rocky beach. At high tide there is no safe place to park seaplanes; landings and takeoffs can be hazardous.

Akhiok has a pleasant, two-teacher school; and children are learning the Aleut language this year through a program sponsored by the Kodiak Area Community Development Corporation. A class in Aleut basket making is also being taught in the village. Working with the village council, KACDC is trying to obtain generators and electrical wiring so Akhiok may be connected with a villagewide electrical system and receive telephone service through the RCA earth station program.

LARSEN BAY

"A great place to go," Larsen Bay has been inhabited for at least the last 2,000 years. Its recent history is tied to the cannery built in 1911 by the Alaska Packers Association. The massive old cannery has been purchased by Kodiak Island Seafoods, Inc., formed by the Old Harbor, Larsen Bay and Karluk village corporations. They plan to operate it on a seasonal basis.

Located on the west shore of Uyak Bay, about 62 air miles west-southwest of Kodiak, Larsen Bay has a population of between 100 and 150. With its protected bay, travel by floatplane and skiff is comparatively easy.

Surrounded by mountains, Larsen Bay is a quiet place with no cars, no roads and is known for its good bear hunting and sports fishing.

The village has no central water system, no sewer system, no airstrip and no electrical distribution system. The houses are old but some have running water, indoor bathrooms and private generators. The village council is working to install a central electrical system and telephones. There is a well-stocked store, post office, and an elementary school affectionately called "the little red schoolhouse." Five or six families live less than 5 minutes across the bay.

Karluk village, with its historic Russian Orthodox church, dates back to Russian occupation. A trading post was founded on the site in 1786. (Gerry Atwell, USF&WS)

Larsen Bay is likely to be the first of the Kodiak Island villages to receive TV beamed by satellite, an event anticipated by envious island residents elsewhere. Said one, in Kodiak, "When it comes we'll have to fly down to Larsen Bay to see anything live."

KARLUK

Even though the last cannery closed 40 years ago, salmon continues to be the mainstay of the economy of Karluk, about 70 miles southwest of the city of Kodiak. The abundance of salmon at Karluk was soon discovered by Russian hunters who later established a trading post there is 1786. Known for many years as the greatest red salmon stream in the world, the 16-mile-long Karluk River—it is said—would be so full that a flat-bottomed skiff could barely navigate through the struggling fish.

Salmon was salted for commercial purposes at Karluk as early as 1870. The first salmon cannery was established on the Karluk spit in 1882 and continued heavy production into the 20th century. Seven canneries operated at Karluk between 1800 and the 1890's; and around 1880 two-thirds of the entire Alaskan salmon pack came from the Karluk River.

Today, locally owned fishing boats are few but most of the men fish during salmon season, either on boats or in beach-seining operations. Some also pack for bear hunters in the fall and spring.

Gust and Freida Reft have a lodge for hunters and fishermen; and Alex Panamaroff Jr. operates the store. Groceries, ordered from Kraft's in Kodiak, are flown in. (One young customer complains a box of Fruit Loops costs $3.20.)

Villagers live in two areas: Old Karluk, northeast of Karluk Lagoon, and New Karluk, on the southwest. The seacoast is extremely rugged with vertical cliffs that fall as much as 500 feet down to the beach. There is "not much of an airstrip and it hasn't been kept up."

Karluk has a church, school and community hall.

Most houses have running water; and some have private generators. Karluk is also on the list for a sewage system, central electrical generation and telephones. Many houses are 50 to 70 years old and were built from secondhand lumber of a still older vintage. "There is a bad fuel problem," an agency spokesman says. "When the oil runs out there is no way to cook, no way to heat your house. No house has insulation. A small house burns three 55-gallon drums of oil per month during winter. At 65 cents a gallon, that's about $120 per house per month. And the house is still cold."

With a small financial base, life is hard in Karluk. But it remains a beautiful place and has a pioneer spirit its 75 to 100 residents are bent on keeping.

Karluk, now with about 100 permanent residents, has subsisted on salmon runs to nearby Karluk Lake for almost 200 years. (Gerry Atwell, USF&WS)

Transparation

Kodiak has come a long way since 1889 when one observer wrote that "there are not ten miles of roadway in all of Alaska outside of . . ." a 13-mile road that encircled nearby Woody Island.

Air transportation to Kodiak is provided by Wien Air Alaska from Anchorage and, on a seasonal basis, by Western Airlines from Seattle. Wien now has once-a-day jet (737) service and uses the propjet 527 on morning flights. During June, July and August, the airline plans jet service for both flights. In 1975, Wien carried approximately 58,000 passengers and hauled approximately 3.5 million pounds of incoming

Upper right — *Runways at Kodiak's major airport, seen from the top of Barometer Mountain. (Gerry Atwell, USF&WS)* Right — *An island highway, temporarily blocked by a landslide. Slides of snow and rocks are frequent on the system of roads. Islanders are accustomed to both the hazards and the delays they cause. (Gary Dobos)*

Top — *A shrimp boat passes though Shelikof Strait. Mountains in the background are on the mainland, part of the Alaska Range. (Gerry Atwell, USF&WS)* Above — *Winter's snows impair travel on the island's roads but add brightness to the countryside. (Jane Elfring)*

freight and mail, and about 1.2 million pounds of outgoing freight and mail.

Kodiak Western Alaska Airlines also serves Kodiak from Anchorage on a charter basis and has scheduled service to Kodiak Island villages. From its base in the Bristol Bay area, the airline also offers regularly scheduled flights from both King Salmon and Dillingham to outlying villages. Weekly service is available originating from Bristol Bay (Tuesday) to Kodiak and (Thursday) from Kodiak to Bristol Bay. During the summer season the company plans flights between the two points three or more times a week.

The summer schedule allows travelers to connect with Western's direct Seattle-to-Kodiak service. The schedule also provides a flight connecting with Reeve Aleutian Airways southbound flight to the Alaska Peninsula and the Aleutian Islands. Charters supplement the scheduled services.

Kodiak Western transports approximately 40,000 passengers and a combined total of four million pounds of freight and mail annually to 21 village communities in the Kodiak Island and Bristol Bay areas.

Additional air taxi service is also available from Air Serv Inc. and Kodiak Air Taxi.

Kodiak's state airport, 7 miles south of town, serves all commercial air carriers, general aviation, the Coast Guard and other military aircraft. The main instrument runway is 7,500 feet long. A new apron and taxiway were completed in 1975 and runway resurfacing in 1976.

The City of Kodiak maintains the 2,800-foot municipal airport in town. The city is applying for federal funds which would allow major improvements such as removing the "hump" in the middle of the runway, installing a lighting system and lengthening Lily Lake 500 feet. This runway and its adjacent lake provide the base of float and wheeled operations for some 40 private aircraft as well as the commercial air taxi operators.

The 296-foot Alaska state ferry M.V. *Tustumena* has linked Kodiak Island with mainland Alaska since the summer of 1964. The ferry now serves Kodiak twice weekly from Homer or Seward, including stops at Port Lions on the north side of Kodiak Island. The ferry can accommodate 200 passengers, including staterooms to sleep 58; and has room for 54 (standard) vehicles. Although the *Tustumena* is only about one-quarter filled during the winter months, reservations are required for travel aboard the ferry in the summer and late fall.

General freight is brought to Kodiak on container vessels by Sea-Land plus occasional visits by Northland Marine Lines. A preferential-use agreement permits Sea-Land to use the city's marine terminal, consisting of one 360-foot wharf with warehouse and one 360-foot wharf and container crane.

—Nancy Freeman

17

Coast Guard Operations

The presence of the U.S. Coast Guard at Kodiak is reassuring to the island communities, all of which depend on air or water travel and make their living from the sea.

Search and rescue (SAR), one of the Coast Guard's most important peace-time missions, covers 1,500,000 square miles in the Kodiak SAR sector, an area roughly half the size of that covered by the lower 48 contiguous states. The Coast Guard Air Station coordinates SAR in the maritime areas bounded by Yakutat on the northeast Gulf of Alaska, Unimak Island in the Aleutians and a northern boundary near Cape Douglas in the Bering Sea. In fiscal 1975, Kodiak Coast Guard SAR reports show 346 cases, 102 lives saved and 653

Upper right — *Twin discs of the White Alice communications system, located on top of 1,270-foot Pillar Mountain. (Gary Dobos)* Right — *Kodiak's U.S. Coast Guard Support Center is the operational base for search and rescue missions and law enforcement across much of the North Pacific. (Jim Hellemn)*

people assisted in operations involving property valued at $25.3 million.

From Kodiak, the unit operates four C-130H long-range fixed-wing aircraft, four HH3F medium-range helicopters and three HH52A short-range helios. By 1980 an additional C-130, two medium-range surveillance aircraft and two additional HH2's are expected.

Although the Coast Guard's major mission is search and rescue, 60% to 70% of its flying time out of Kodiak is devoted to fisheries patrols called Alaska Patrols or Alpats in support of U.S. law and treaties. These patrols vary from surveillance of foreign fishing fleets to marine environmental protection. Logistics flights are made to supply various outlying Coast Guard installations.

A vital 24-hour link with the outside world is provided by the Coast Guard's communications station, which monitors international distress frequencies and broadcasts weather and notices to mariners.

Three ships are home-ported at the Kodiak Coast Guard Support Center: the cutters *Storis, Confidence* and *Citrus*. Both the *Storis* and *Confidence* give surface search and rescue assistance, logistics support, and make law enforcement patrols in support of U.S. treaties. The cutter *Confidence* is also equipped to land and refuel the HH52A helios. The primary mission of the cutter *Citrus* is servicing aids to navigation in and around Kodiak Island, Afognak Island, the Shelikof Strait and south shore of the Alaskan Peninsula. The *Citrus* is also frequently called upon to assist in SAR and law enforcement. Other Coast Guard vessels occasionally supplement locally based ships in the Alpat efforts.

The Coast Guard Support Center, about 4 miles southwest of the city of Kodiak, provides facilities and services to the tenant commands and dependents of Coast Guard personnel assigned to the area. The Coast Guard also operates a 15-bed hospital, serving more than 2,700 active-duty military, retired military and dependents.

With a population of 2,300 (including dependents) and an annual payroll of $12 million in 1976, the Coast Guard facility at Kodiak is the largest in Alaska. And it is growing. Partly because of its added enforcement responsibility with the passage of the federal 200-mile-limit law, the Coast Guard will build 168 housing units to handle expected increases in personnel. This project, plus a complete rehabilitation of two hangars, pier facilities, utilities and barracks, will cost approximately $34.5 million. The Coast Guard will spend another $3.5 million to build a loran-C station as an aid to navigation at Narrow Cape. Both projects will draw manpower from the civilian community and contribute significantly to the local economy.

18

The Awesome Barrens

Buffetted by unpredictable, frequently violent winds and awash during storms, the Latax Rocks and Barren Islands group are still home to some 700,000 sea birds. The name for Latax Rocks was derived from the Aleut word for the sea otters which inhabit the area. Captain James Cook named the Barren Islands May 25, 1778.

According to a final environmental statement prepared on proposed "Alaska Coastal National Wildlife Refuges," the Department of the Interior is recommending the establishment of the Barren Islands National Wildlife Refuge. Islands in this proposal rise from the Gulf of Alaska near the entrance to Cook Inlet. Latax Rocks are a few miles offshore from Shuyak Island and 15 miles north of Afognak Island. The Barren Islands are about 17 miles northeast of Latax Rocks between Shuyak Island and the Kenai Peninsula.

"The 188 islets and islands in this

proposal encompass the most important known nesting areas for their size in a 1,000-mile arc along the Gulf of Alaska," the report says.

Latax Rocks are about 20 acres with the largest islet just 8 acres in size and only 32 feet above mean sea level. Even access by boat is difficult.

Islands of the mountainous Barren Islands dot an area 15 miles long by 6 miles wide and include six major islands and many lesser islands and rocks with a total land area of 10,000 acres. East Amatuli and West Amatuli Islands rise to heights of 1,539 and 1,360 feet respectively. Both are precipitous, with bold headlands, ideal sites for nesting marine birds.

Nord, Sud and Sugarloaf Islands are conic in shape, rising 690, 980 and 1,210 feet, respectively. Ushagat Island, largest of the Barren group at 6,800 acres, rises to a height of 1,935 feet. Its northern side slopes into a large, low bowl containing a brackish lake. A few collapsed cabins on Ushagat and Sud Islands date to the era of fox farming in the early 1900's. Activity stopped on Sud Island with the expiration of a fur farm lease in 1939.

Sea lion populations in the Barren Islands have fluctuated between 8,000 and 12,000 animals for many years. An estimated 4,000 pups were born in rookeries there in 1971. Harbor seals probably range between 500 and 1,000 animals and sea otters between 400 and 600 animals.

Despite their small size, the Latax Rocks and the adjacent shoals and reefs are an excellent marine mammal area.

Heavy concentrations of black-legged kittiwakes nest on Nord Island, one of the smallest of the Barrens. (Ed Bailey, reprinted from ALASKA® magazine)

An estimated 3,300 sea lions, 500 or more harbor seals and 200 to 300 sea otters use the area. Both sea lions and seals have been harvested in the Barren Islands. In 1971 hunters harvested 1,008 sea lions. The moratorium on marine mammal hunting has halted the activity.

The hundreds of thousands of birds that nest on the islands include the black-legged kittiwake, tufted puffin, parakeet auklet, common murre, thick-billed murre, horned puffin, fulmar, pelagic cormorant and fewer hundreds of black oystercatcher, red-faced cormorant, fork-tailed petrel, marbled murrelet, ancient murrelet and crested auklet.

Because access to these islands is hazardous, they have been mostly left to the birds.

19

The Other Islands

Chirikof Island, bottom line of the archipelago, is about 160 miles southwest of Kodiak. Called everything from foggy, lonely, isolated and desolate in the last 200 years, the island once held Russian prisoners. The penal colony was disbanded in 1871 and the 30 people there were allowed to go wherever they wanted—and many reportedly spread out to Kodiak Island villages.

The island's remoteness has blocked a number of successive cattle ranching attempts, and the "Isle of Doom" has been a party to more than its share of tragedy. In 1967, for example, two Kodiak men who had planned to bring back a load of beef from Chirikof were killed when their aircraft failed to gain altitude, flipped and burned.

Isolated strips of shoreline collect discards from the sea, everything from once-proud fishing vessels to glass floats from Japanese fishing nets. (Guy Powell, Commercial Fish Division, ADF&G)

Raspberry Island, 82 square miles and about 20 minutes by air west of the city of Kodiak, sees little human activity until summer when some 10 to 12 gill-net sites are in operation. Once the location of an old herring plant, Raspberry more recently was the site of Wakefield Fisheries (old Port Wakefield) before the 1964 earthquake and tidal wave. Land subsidence and subsequent damaging high tides made it necessary to move the facilities to the "new" village of Port Lions in 1967. Raspberry has no year-round residents at present, but supports beaver, red squirrels, parka squirrels, deer and an elk population.

Sitkalidak Island, third largest in the Kodiak group, was the site of the Port Hobron whaling station in the 1800's. A number of cattle ventures have occurred on the island. Among the more famous was a large ranch master-minded by the late Jack McCord, who also is credited with persuading Congress in 1925-26 to enact the law which permits the leasing of federally owned land in Alaska for grazing and fur farming.

Sitkinak, part of the Trinity Islands group at the southwest tip of Kodiak Island, has also sustained cattle since the mid-1900's. A cattle ranching operation is currently under way. A Coast Guard loran station is also located on the island.

Tugidak, "a flat little island that sits out there by itself," at the southern tip of Kodiak Island, is home for thousands of harbor seals. About 71 square miles and only a few feet above sea level, the island is reportedly good for goose hunting in the fall and has an abundance of parka squirrels. No one lives there at this time.

20

Ranching Kodiak Style

Millions of acres of forage and reports of cattle "fat as seals" have long attracted ranchers to the prospects of the Kodiak archipelago. The Russians are credited with bringing the first cattle, a Siberian breed, to Kodiak Island before 1790.

Writer/historian C. L. Andrews wrote Alexander Baranof "introduced cattle at Kodiak. . .and there were 500 head of cattle [there] during his time [1791-1818]." (Andrews, "Alaska under the Russians," 1916.)

Sixty years later, "There may be 50 head of cattle on [Kodiak] island and as many more on Woody Island," wrote George Wardman in *Trip to Alaska*, 1884. "More cattle are found here than in any other portion of Alaska, though hay must be provided for their support during four months of the year."

And getting the hay was never easy.

Horses and cattle still cluster on Kodiak's flats to search for the first sprigs of spring's green grass. (Gary Dobos)

A turn-of-the-century view of the Kodiak Agricultural Experiment Station. Pictured are Harry White, left, and W. T. White. W. T. White Jr., in the carriage, is now a Kodiak businessman. (University of Alaska Archives, Fairbanks)

Above — *Driftwood corrals limit the range of horses on remote Chirikof Island, southwest of the Trinity Group. (Guy Powell, Commercial Fish Division ADF&G)* Left — *Herefords are among the hearty breeds that prosper on Kodiak's native grasses. (Gary Dobos)*

Schoolteacher Robert G. Slifer, in a letter dated August 5, 1899, told his beloved:

"One day this week I was over to Long Island helping them make hay for the winter there. There all the grass is cut with scythes, dried and then wrapped in fish nets and carried to the barn on your back. . . . The grass was thin and tough and you had to use a great deal of force with the scythe to get it off and it almost used us all up. It rained on Friday and so our work was stopped but I may go over again next week. They pay $1.50 a day and board and that is not to be despised when a fellow has nothing to do, I'll tell you."

To provide hay for the Baptist Mission stock (on Woody Island), Slifer said, "we cut it in Kalsinsky Bay, about 15 miles from here. . . ." Troubled twice with bad seas, "once going down we were caught by a head wind and rowed till 1:30 in the morning till we could get a good place to land and I tell you, I was tired. . . .

"We cut the grass off the 'flats' at low tide, stacked it in heaps and then

85

Above — *Cattle breeders have experimented with a variety of European cattle, including Scottish Highlands and Galloways, that were thought to be more adaptable to Kodiak's environment than U.S. breeds. This animal appears to trace its ancestry to Scotland. (Randy Weisser)* Right — *Calves gathered for branding at the Kodiak Cattle Company ranch.* Far right — *Roundup at the Kodiak Cattle Company. The ranch runs about 600 head of Angus and Herefords. (Both photos, Suzanne Manolovitz)*

86

piled it into boats and poled it down the river when the tides were higher and loaded it into a scow; and a little steam launch then towed the scow home. . . . I was down the greater part of three weeks altogether and we got about 40 tons of ensilage. You can know how important it is that they gather this food for the stock when I tell you that last winter hay was worth $42 a ton here and that it had to be carried on your back as well as being cut down and raked up by hand. . . .''

A U. S. Department of Agriculture experiment station was established on Kodiak Island in 1906 with a herd of Galloway cattle. At about the same time, C. H. Frye had a large stock farm at Kodiak "where a dozen horses, 200 cattle and 200 sheep thrive, increase and keep fat the year through on native feed, consisting of beach grass, blue top, timothy and willow. A small amount of hay and silage is prepared for feed at such times as the snow may cover the winter pasture. Frost may be expected about September first."

The Frye-Bruhn Cattle Company was near the present site of the Coast Guard Air Station. "During the winter of 1903, the company lost 140 head of cattle, mostly by falling over the cliffs."

By 1946 it was reported "one large dairy is near the Naval Base on Kodiak Island [a quart of milk was already 40 cents]. . . . The main beef cattle herds are on Kodiak Island [others were on Sitkalidak and Chirikof]. . . . The flocks of sheep are concentrated apparently on Sitkalidak, Unalaska and Umnak Islands.''

The same analyst said "The most favored locations for straight range livestock production are on Kodiak and adjacent islands and on the Aleutians. . . . Three moderate sized beef-cattle herds, one large dairy herd and several head of saddle horses are maintained on Kodiak Island. . . . A limited quantity of grass hay and silage is produced for wintering beef cows and calves on Kodiak Island, but the remaining range livestock and the herds on the other islands survive on native [grasses] alone.''

"The grass—the basic resource—is still there," a Kodiak rancher says, "and how to use it economically is still the challenge."

Total range lands for the island group are estimated at 3.3 million acres, which includes the higher elevations of sparse but high-quality grazing. Grazing leases cover 355,000 acres and support about 4,500 cattle. Northeastern Kodiak Island, an area of 307,200 acres, contains 101,860 acres considered suitable for grazing. The remaining acreage is barren or inaccessible to livestock. As of January 1973, 137,190 acres of the area were under grazing leases carrying about 1,350 cattle, 120 sheep and 50 horses.

Beef and veal production in the western gulf area have averaged 132 metric tons yearly from 1965 to 1972 with an average yearly value of $140,000. During 1972 production amounted to 121 metric tons and was valued at $150,000 according to the Alaska Crop and Livestock Reporting Service. Most of the beef produced on Kodiak Island

is processed at the Kodiak Livestock Co-op Processing Plant and is sold as locker beef. Additional cattle from the islands south of the Alaska Peninsula have also been processed at the Kodiak facility.

The potential productivity of the grazing lands for beef, particularly on Kodiak, Tugidak, Sitkinak and Chirikof Islands has been acclaimed by many, but actual range surveys have been limited to Kodiak Island.

And food value of the forage on Kodiak Island varies considerably with the season. During winter, pasture grass is of very poor quality, and herds graze along the beaches, especially around the bays or inlets. While the cattle have almost unlimited grazing range in summer, they are in danger from bears. Cattle mortality is highest during March and April and has been attributed to malnutrition, bear depredation, falls from precipitous slopes and poisonous plants.

Kodiak's pioneer ranchers are also facing colder winters, rising freight rates and expiring leases. What sustains them is a highly individualized lifestyle and the sight of grass-fattened beef on their way to market.

Left — *The late Charles Madsen, one of the most famous Kodiak bear guides, outfitted for a hunt in the 1930's. (Eli Metrokin)* Above — *Bear guide Alf Madsen with an 11-foot, 8-inch by 10-foot, 2-inch trophy bear taken in 1953. (Kodiak Historical Society)* Below — *Early-century hunters return with a trophy between them. (Erskine Collection, University of Alaska Archives, Fairbanks)*

21

A Bear Economy

Although one of Kodiak Island's less visible industries, the business of guiding hunters in pursuit of Kodiak brown bear adds nearly $750,000 to the local economy each year. The annual average bear take in the Kodiak area (Unit 8) is 136 animals, but the activity involves many more hunters. From 1970 through 1974, an average of 124 nonresidents received hunting permits for the Kodiak Island Wildlife Refuge, while probably another 30 nonresidents hunted outside those boundaries.

Talking about people from outside Alaska only, Roger Smith, area game management biologist, sets the average annual figure conservatively at 150 who are guided for "as cheaply as $1,500 or for as much as $3,700." If the nonresident pays an average of $2,800, the bears annually bring in more that $400,000 in guide fees. Not included are transportation costs from almost anywhere in the world to Kodiak Island and

Top — *Hunter-trapper Walter Metrokin, described by* National Geographic *magazine as "the celebrated one-handed bear hunter of Kodiak." Metrokin also participated in* Geographic *expeditions to Mount Katmai following the 1912 eruption.* Above — *Charles Madsen's Karluk Lake tent camp for hunters in the 1930's. (Both photos, Eli Metrokin)*

back, or the nearly $200 required for nonresident hunting licenses and big game tags. Directly or indirectly, these out-of-state hunters annually leave behind some $750,000.

Few Alaska residents hire guides for bear hunts but a growing number are traveling from Anchorage and Fairbanks for the Kodiak hunt. "As Alaska's population increases in the urban areas," Smith predicts, "guides will start booking more residents."

Interestingly enough, non-Alaskans with professional guides have a success rate of 70% or better, Smith says, while the figure drops to less than 50% for a local hunter on his own. He explains that "brown bear require a fairly sophisticated type of hunting and are not as abundant as other big game species."

Hunters ill-prepared for fickle weather and what can be a harsh and alien land may spend most of their time trying to survive the elements.

Hunters apply to the Alaska Department of Fish and Game for permits under a new system that includes drawings for the spring and fall hunts and separate drawings for residents and nonresidents.

Another change is the creation of the Guide Licensing and Control Board, already credited with strengthening a code of ethics for guiding practices. The board also has established exclusive areas for big game guides. In practice, "there has been only a small reduction in the number of guides (19 are now registered) because most guides who have been active here in the last five years have received some guiding area." While some guides complain about shorter seasons and the restrictions of being scrunched up in a particular area, most feel bears are well protected.

Smith estimates the guides have about 20 to 25 actual hunting days during each of the fall and spring hunts. Almost all the areas within the Kodiak unit (including Afognak, Shuyak and Raspberry Islands) open March 1 through May 20; but in the fall, the Afognak season extends from October 1, while the opening date for most of the Kodiak Island group is October 25 through December 31.

Bears are one of the most intensively managed big game species in Alaska, Smith says. "The department looks at specimens from virtually every bear taken in the state." Hunters are required to bring bear hides and skulls to the nearest Fish and Game office for measurement, and a tooth is extracted from the skull to determine the animal's age. Studies of the hides, skulls and teeth of animals harvested over the last 5 years indicate that the brown bear population is reasonably stable, Smith says. "If there were any evidence of a declining number of bears, we would immediately reduce hunting."

With the unpredictability of Kodiak weather, the ever-flexing rules and changing patterns of landownership, guiding surely attracts a special kind of man.

"I like to compare it to bullfighting," one guide says, "you never know what's going to come out of the chute."

What wonder then that these Nantucketers, born on a beach should take to the sea for a livelihood. They first caught crabs and quahogs in the sand; grown bolder, they waded out with nets for mackerel; more experienced, they pushed off in boats and captured cod; and at last, launching a Navy of great ships on the sea, explored this watery world; put an incessant belt of circumnavigation round it; peeped in at Bhering's Straits; and in all seasons and all oceans declared everlasting war with the mightiest mass that has survived the flood; most monstrous and most mountainous!

Commercial Fishing, Economic Mainstay

These words, borrowed from Melville's *Moby Dick,* well describe the developing mood of the Kodiak fishing industry,'' says Captain Dave Kennedy, Kodiak fisherman and instructor at Kodiak Community College. "Fishermen from other areas and fish industry representatives new to Kodiak say there is something different about the Kodiak fisherman. There's a compelling force that drives him, and it is like a whirlpool that draws others. Some say the Kodiak fisherman is well informed; others argue that he is misinformed. All agree he is outspoken, interested in his future and competitive within his industry.''

It is this competitiveness, Kennedy feels, that has kept Kodiak among the top three ports in the nation for value of

Left — *Arnold Ingvald Haram Jr. gaffs a 15-pound halibut aboard the schooner* North *off the Semidi Islands, southwest of Kodiak.* (Tom Casey)

fishery products landed, and number one for products landed from its own coastal waters. Kodiak landings were worth $252 million retail in 1974. This included 36% of the total Alaska harvest of shellfish. In 1975, Kodiak fishermen caught 23.6 million pounds of king crab; 25.5 million pounds of tanner crab; 48.8 million pounds of shrimp; 780,000 pounds of Dungeness crab; 148,000 pounds of scallops; 198,000 pounds of razor clams; 5 million pounds of halibut; 3.5 million pounds of salmon; and thousands of pounds of other species.

"The future looks bright; and there is a *great* potential in bottomfish. The foreign fleets harvested between 220 and 280 million pounds of bottomfish from the coastal waters of Kodiak Island in 1975," Kennedy says. "When the challenge presents itself, Kodiak is ready."

Tom Casey, manager of the United Fishermen's Marketing Association in Kodiak and formerly a fisherman, describes the ocean fishermen of the Gulf of Alaska and the Bering Sea this way:

"These men earn their money long-lining for halibut, trawling for shrimp and pot-fishing for king crab and tanner crab. They are restless and independent; bound to shore only temporarily by a spring line or two half hitches. Alaska fishermen work for a living

Iceman aboard the F.V. Captain Joe *shovels flake ice onto fresh shrimp. The vessel carries about 20 tons of flake ice on each voyage, enough to successfully store 200,000 pounds of shrimp, the anticipated catch in 2 to 4 days of fishing. (Tom Casey)*

The cod end of the port-side trawl will drop about 8,000 pounds of shrimp on the deck of double-rigged trawler Captain Joe. *Catch from an earlier drag is already on deck. (Tom Casey)*

. . . all day and, very often, all night. They don't punch a time clock and they don't get weekends and holidays off. The bounds of their exertion are the dimensions of their fish hold. As soon as they fill it up, they relax . . . for a while.

"The successful Alaska fisherman is a composite of various talents. His dependence upon winches, motors and diesel engines, forces him to master many mechanical skills. Malfunctions of his navigation and fishing equipment frequently challenge his electronic ability. Fluctuations in market demand for his fish, currency exchange rates, and national rates of inflation rapidly convert the novice fisherman into an efficient, cost-conscious businessman . . . or a bankrupt former fisherman.

"Modern ocean fishing," Casey continues, "is strictly business in Alaska. Multimillion-dollar vessels, high interest rates, 42-cents-per-gallon diesel fuel, place relentless demands upon a captain's ability to catch fish and the crew's ability to properly handle and preserve what the captain provides.

"On April 13, 1976, when President Ford signed the 200-mile limit law, Alaska fishermen became world citizens. In 1974 foreign fishermen harvested nearly 5.5 billion pounds of fish and shellfish from the Gulf of Alaska and the Bering Sea. Much of that was an overharvest. That same year, American fishermen landed approximately 0.5 billion pounds of fish and shellfish along Alaska's coast. At the time, no legal means existed to enforce conservation measures applied to the foreign fleets. Likewise, there was no mechan-

View from the pilothouse of the king crab vessel Amatuli *working in a 30-mph wind and a quartering sea in the Bering Sea. (Bart Eaton)*

ism that could be used to enlarge the Alaskan domestic catch while steadily reducing the gigantic foreign harvest.

"Circumstances are different now," Casey says. "The 200-mile limit law mandates strict conservation of all American coastal and anadromous fish stocks and provides the legal 'teeth' to guarantee foreign fishermen's compliance with catch quotas established by federal councils and the Secretary of Commerce. Additionally, the 200-mile limit law arms Alaskan fishermen with a powerful 'preferential-right' principle that grants Alaskan fishermen first crack at any available fish quota. If Alaskan fishermen demonstrate the capability and desire to harvest the entire available quota, no foreign fishing may occur on that fish stock. This preferential-right principle may well lead Alaskan fishermen to domination of the Gulf of Alaska and the eastern Bering Sea fisheries.

"And yet, to most Americans, ocean fishermen remain strangers. The Barnacle Bill stereotype is a common impression Americans still have of their fishermen: Old salts with corncob pipes, a black eyepatch, wearing red-checkered woolen shirt and gray trousers and a yellow sou'wester, who row out in a dory and jig for halibut or trawl aboard an ancient, weather-beaten schooner for codfish.

"Little do most Americans realize how heavily they may eventually rely upon their fishermen for future protein from the sea. It is well known that world agricultural production is dependent upon large amounts of fresh water and natural-gas-derived fertilizers. The world supply of natural gas could last another 30 years at the current rate of industrial consumption. It is likely, therefore, that the supply of natural-gas-based fertilizers will continually decline. Unless alternative sources of fertilizer can be found, world meat and grain production will be undermined. And the diet of the world's population will have to be supplemented by greater amounts of marine protein. Who is most likely to provide that fish protein? Not Barnacle Bill, you can be sure.

"Most likely the same Alaskan fishermen who trawl the North Pacific and the Bering Sea. Largely anonymous now, they may soon become the object of national attention and pride. For these reasons, Americans must become better acquainted with their fishermen. The first step is to show Americans who their fishermen really are, what a modern fishing vessel can accomplish and what savage weather men and vessels must withstand in the course of their work.

"Fishing towns, fishing vessels, the high seas fertile with all varieties of fish—this is the fisherman's world. And he stands at the center of it."

—*Nancy Freeman*

93

And Now Petroleum

Above — *An orange nudibranch, center, below a branchiopod and surrounded by feeding brown coral. Right — Colonial red coral flanked by colonial brownish coral. Purple, encrusting coraline algae covers local rock surfaces. A pile of shell from deceased mollusks is nearby. (All photos of Kodiak's underwater life in this chapter, Guy Powell, Commercial Fish Division, ADF&G)*

The outer continental shelf oil lease sales scheduled for the Kodiak area may be delayed but there has never been a scheduled OCS sale that has not taken place. Oil is inevitable. No one seems to doubt there are large petroleum reserves off these islands; and it also appears that Kodiak may be Alaska's first coastal community to have its feet on the ground in advance of oil production.

The Outer Continental Shelf Advisory Council (OCS task force) created by Kodiak Island Borough—bolstered with a $36,000 state-federal grant, plus $18,000 in-kind help from the borough—is preparing a base-line study to determine "where we are now. . .somehow predict what normal growth would be without oil and impose the OCS growth curve on top of that to determine Kodiak's total future needs for goods and services."

Some of the question marks are how much petroleum is in the Kodiak shelf;

where is it located; how much will be sold; and when will it be developed? A preliminary study to estimate offshore exploration and development prepared by Alaska's Division of Geological and Geophysical Surveys is being updated. However, the report makes several assumptions that may stand the test of time.

For starters, "the acreage proposed for leasing on the outer continental shelf near Kodiak supports the most intensive and valuable shellfish fisheries in Alaskan waters, is a prime habitat for major populations of herring, salmon, sea birds, and marine mammals and includes major domestic and foreign fishing grounds. The coastal waters are essential as breeding and nursery areas for the eight Alaskan crab and shrimp species of commercial importance; fishing for these species occurs in both coastal and offshore waters. There are regions of extreme seismic risk within the proposed lease area, including the zone of major vertical displacement during the 1964 earthquake."

Although the lease sale for the general area was earlier announced for December 1976, the Secretary of the Interior is reviewing the entire planning schedule for Alaska and date of the Kodiak sale has yet to be confirmed.

And while the lease area has been reduced to a quarter of what was originally available for nomination by the petroleum industry, "the other three-quarters could be included in future lease sales," speculates a state employee. "We can't say it will be or it won't be; that depends directly upon the success of the original lease."

Annelid worms display multicolored gills. The animals, surrounded here by a mat of sponges, feed on plankton and organic matter carried to them by ocean currents.

A nudibranch's feathery fringe along the body is used for respiration. The animal is also known as a "naked snail."

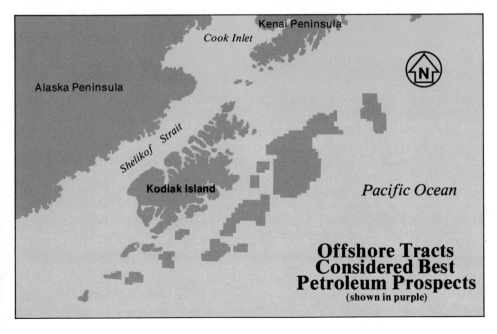

Kenai Peninsula
Cook Inlet
Alaska Peninsula
Shelikof Strait
Kodiak Island
Pacific Ocean

Offshore Tracts Considered Best Petroleum Prospects
(shown in purple)

95

A marine community found beneath a piece of shale: a 1-year-old king crab, surrounded by clams, urchins, brittle stars, sea stars, snails and hermit crabs.

The Department of the Interior has tentatively selected 3.2 million acres, involving 564 tracts, most to the northeast of the city of Kodiak, for intensive environmental analysis. Following the preparation of a draft environmental impact statement, the Department of the Interior and the Bureau of Land Management will schedule public hearings, another time for public input into the decision-making process.

Because "there are areas of the northwest Gulf of Alaska shelf that possess the highest of values from the standpoint of renewable resources, that have an intensive human-use factor and an extreme biological sensitivity," the State of Alaska has recommended to the Bureau of Land Management that approximately 696 tracts within the area, designated as "high industry interest," be withheld from leasing.

The preliminary study assumes petroleum reserves estimated at from a low of 372 million barrels of oil and 2.3 billion cubic feet of gas to a high estimate of 2.5 billion barrels of oil and 8 trillion cubic feet of gas. Further assumed is there will be 5-year leases in the Kodiak area with exploratory drilling expected to begin in 1977 and continue through 1982 to validate the leases.

Koniag, Inc., the regional Native corporation, is proposing that the former Cape Chiniak Air Force Tracking Station (now closed and received by Koniag) be used by the oil companies for an exploratory support base, thereby reducing the impact on the city of Kodiak, 42 miles distant. Also proposed is that the Cape Chiniak harbor be the base for supply boats needed to shuttle equipment and water to the semisubmersible drilling rigs. In addition to supply boats, each semisubmersible rig requires one helicopter about the size of a Bell 204. The helicopters act as sky buses, shuttling crew and company executives from shore to the rigs.

Estimating the minimum economic size of a prospect at 300 million barrels, the study assumes at least a single field (low estimate) at a minimum of 300 million barrels. A high estimate calls for five fields at 300 million barrels apiece and two other fields rated at 500 million barrels. There will most likely be two production platforms per field with between 25 and 40 wells drilled per platform.

How long will it take? In the shortest time frame, the study says, 6 months for engineering the first platform; 1 year to construct the platform in the shipyard. If it is built in San Francisco, 1 to 2 months to tow it to the Kodiak shelf. Once the platform is on site, another construction period will be needed to install modules and producing and drilling equipment on the platform base.

Low and high estimates place exploration drilling from 1977 through 1982, estimating the first production platform will be set on location between 1980 and 1983. Initial oil production is predicted to begin between 1982 and 1985, with peak production between 1991 and 1994.

Kodiak has heard reports that "the exploration, development and production of oil and gas on the nearby continental shelf could represent at least 6,000 new direct jobs and a financial investment of $15 billion. It could create another 6,000 indirect jobs, compared to the total nonmilitary employment of Kodiak which in 1974 was 4,400 persons." The same report estimated population growth at 6,000 to 25,000 depending on the size of the oil field play, if any at all.

Others speculate that the population impact from offshore oil development will proceed at a slower pace and total only an additional few hundred in the Kodiak area.

With or without oil, "Kodiak will be changing and changing fast," comments an observer. "Projected population statistics alone show that. From a current level of 9,000-plus, Kodiak's population at the end of this century is predicted to jump to 23,000—without oil development.

"After the fisheries, government provides the next biggest source of employment [not including the Coast Guard] and, with the increase in population, government services and workers to administer them will grow apace."

What concerns the community is protection of its renewable marine resources, perpetuation of the unique lifestyle of its people; and assurance that old and young can continue to enjoy Kodiak as a place relatively free from crowding, crime and pollution.

—*Nancy Freeman*